CIPS STUDY MATTERS

ADVANCED CERTIFICATE
IN PROCUREMENT AND SUPPLY OPERATIONS

COURSE BOOK

Inventory and logistics operations

© Profex Publishing Limited, 2012

Printed and distributed by:

The Chartered Institute of Purchasing & Supply, Easton House, Easton on the Hill, Stamford, Lincolnshire
PE9 3NZ
Tel: +44 (0) 1780 756 777
Fax: +44 (0) 1780 751 610
Email: info@cips.org
Website: www.cips.org

First edition September 2012

Contents

Preface

Welcome to your new Course Book.

Your Course Book provides detailed coverage of all topics specified in the unit content.

For a full explanation of how to use your new Course Book, turn now to page ix. And good luck in your studies!

A note on style

Throughout your Course Books you will find that we use the masculine form of personal pronouns. This convention is adopted purely for the sake of stylistic convenience – we just don't like saying 'he/she' all the time. Please don't think this reflects any kind of bias or prejudice.

September 2012

The Unit Content

The unit content is reproduced below, together with reference to the chapter in this Course Book where each topic is covered.

Unit characteristics

On completion of this unit, candidates will be able to select appropriate techniques to ensure the right inventory can be purchased or supplied.

This unit focuses on the techniques that can be applied to achieve the availability of inventories through the flow of materials and information.

Learning outcomes, assessment criteria and indicative content

Chapter

1.0 Understand the main implications of purchasing and supplying inventory

1.1 Classify the main types of inventory

• Definitions of inventory and inventory stock management	1
• Opening stock, work in progress and finished goods	1
• Safety stocks	1

1.2 Assess the costs involved in holding inventory

• Acquisition and holding costs	2
• Methods for the valuation of inventory such as LIFO, FIFO, average cost and standard cost	2
• The profit and loss entry of cost of sales and goods sold	2
• The balance sheet entry for inventory	2

1.3 Explain the main techniques for the monitoring and control of inventory

• Pareto analysis and ABC classifications of inventory	3
• Dependent and independent demand	3
• MRP and MRPII	3
• Just in time supply and *kanban* systems	3
• Consignment stocking and vendor managed inventory	3

1.4 Analyse the main techniques for calculating the future demand of inventory

• Economic order quantity	4
• Reorder point and periodic review systems	4
• MRP and MRPII	4
• The bullwhip effect	4
• Service levels for inventory and working with sales and marketing	1
• Qualitative and quantitative approaches to forecasting	4

How to Use Your Course Book

Organising your study

'Organising' is the key word: unless you are a very exceptional student, you will find a haphazard approach is insufficient, particularly if you are having to combine study with the demands of a full-time job.

A good starting point is to timetable your studies, in broad terms, between now and the date of your assessment. How many subjects are you attempting? How many chapters are there in the Course Book for each subject? Now do the sums: how many days/weeks do you have for each chapter to be studied?

Remember:

- Not every week can be regarded as a study week – you may be going on holiday, for example, or there may be weeks when the demands of your job are particularly heavy. If these can be foreseen, you should allow for them in your timetabling.
- You also need a period leading up to the assessment in which you will revise and practise what you have learned.

Once you have done the calculations, make a week-by-week timetable for yourself for each paper, allowing for study and revision of the entire unit content between now and the date of your assessment.

Getting started

Aim to find a quiet and undisturbed location for your study, and plan as far as possible to use the same period each day. Getting into a routine helps avoid wasting time. Make sure you have all the materials you need before you begin – keep interruptions to a minimum.

Using the Course Book

You should refer to the Course Book to the extent that you need it.

- If you are a newcomer to the subject, you will probably need to read through the Course Book quite thoroughly. This will be the case for most students.
- If some areas are already familiar to you – either through earlier studies or through your practical work experience – you may choose to skip sections of the Course Book.

The content of the Course Book

This Course Book has been designed to give detailed coverage of every topic in the unit content. As you will see from pages vii–viii, each topic mentioned in the unit content is dealt with in a chapter of the Course Book. For the most part the order of the Course Book follows the order of the unit content closely, though departures from this principle have occasionally been made in the interest of a logical learning order.

Each chapter begins with a reference to the assessment criteria and unit content to be covered in the chapter. Each chapter is divided into sections, listed in the introduction to the chapter, and for the most part being actual captions from the unit content.

All of this enables you to monitor your progress through the unit content very easily and provides reassurance that you are tackling every subject that is examinable.

Each chapter contains the following features.

- Clear coverage of each topic in a concise and approachable format
- A chapter summary
- Self-test questions

The study phase

For each chapter you should begin by glancing at the main headings (listed at the start of the chapter). Then read fairly rapidly through the body of the text to absorb the main points. If it's there in the text, you can be sure it's there for a reason, so try not to skip unless the topic is one you are familiar with already.

Then return to the beginning of the chapter to start a more careful reading. You may want to take brief notes as you go along.

Test your recall and understanding of the material by attempting the self-test questions. These are accompanied by cross-references to paragraphs where you can check your answers and refresh your memory.

The revision phase

Your approach to revision should be methodical and you should aim to tackle each main area of the unit content in turn. Re-read your notes. Then do some question practice. The CIPS website contains many past exam questions and you should aim to identify those that are suitable for the unit you are studying.

Additional reading

Your Course Book provides you with the key information needed for each module but CIPS strongly advocates reading as widely as possible to augment and reinforce your understanding. CIPS produces an official reading list of books, which can be downloaded from the bookshop area of the CIPS website.

To help you, we have identified one essential textbook for each subject. We recommend that you read this for additional information.

The essential textbook for this unit is *Purchasing and Supply Chain Management* by Kenneth Lysons and Brian Farrington.

CHAPTER 1

Classifying Inventory

Assessment criteria and indicative content

1.1 Classify the main types of inventory

- Definitions of inventory and inventory stock management
- Opening stock, work in progress and finished goods
- Safety stocks

1.4 Analyse the main techniques for calculating the future demand of inventory

- Service levels for inventory and working with sales and marketing

Section headings

1 Definitions
2 Reasons for holding stock
3 Customer service and availability

1 Definitions

Classifying stocks by type

1.1 Most organisations hold stocks of one kind or another. The groups and categories of stock may be described in a number of ways and the description is likely to depend on the organisation in which the stock is kept. However, there is potentially a long list of stock categories and we describe some of these in this first section of the chapter. Many of our examples refer to the manufacturing environment, which is characterised by a high level of stockholding, but other categories of stock may be held by any kind of organisation.

1.2 **Raw materials** – these would be prime materials in their raw state entering the production process of a manufacturing organisation. The nature of the raw materials would depend upon the company's products. Examples would include steel and aluminium in a manufacturer of car bodies, or water, malt and hops in a brewery.

1.3 **Components** – these are complete parts in their own right but destined to be incorporated into the manufacturing process. Examples include fixings, 'O' rings, switches, cases/frames, bearings, etc. Again, the actual nature of the components will depend on the nature of the manufactured product.

1.4 **Subassemblies** – these are partly assembled or manufactured parts moving through the assembly chain. They are often purchased ready assembled from suppliers. Examples would include gearboxes and suspension units for car manufacture.

1.5   **Work in progress** – this is partly finished work which can incorporate raw materials, components and subassemblies moving forward in the production process. These items often require storage because it is impossible to complete the production process in one smooth flow. For example, this might happen if a production line is used for part of the production process and then has to be stopped so that the machines can be adjusted to complete the process. Once the adjustment has taken place, production would continue using the work in progress stocks.

1.6   **Consumable stores** – these are used in a manufacturing process but without becoming part of the final product. Examples are lubricants, solvents, foundry sand etc. In fact this kind of stock is common outside the manufacturing environment as well. All organisations require consumables such as stationery, 'janitorial' supplies and office equipment.

1.7   **Tools** – a manufacturing organisation will hold stocks of tools, jigs and fixtures to fabricate or manufacture the products, eg taps and dies, press tools, moulds, etc.

1.8   **Machine spares** – these are items required for maintenance of the capital equipment within the business. This category of stock is sometimes thought of as being related only to manufacturing concerns but it can relate to any organisation that uses machines. It is particularly important to carry stocks of spares in situations where machines may break down suddenly. Preventive maintenance cannot always rule out sudden breakdowns and for such situations emergency spares should always be stocked. Quantities need not be too great, however. Many organisations stock just two emergency spares of an item and when one is used, simply replace it immediately. A simple example is a toner cartridge for a laser printer.

1.9   **Packaging materials** – typically, these would be retail or wholesale outer packaging materials, cases and wraps. Returnable packing cases and fixtures, together with their associated wrapping materials for distribution, might also be included.

1.10   **Marketing materials** – most organisations will keep stocks of catalogues, sales data sheets, promotional literature, etc.

1.11   **Finished goods** – products in their wrapping ready for sale. Many companies need to keep comprehensive stocks of finished products so that they can satisfy customer orders without delay. The ability to do this might keep them ahead of their competitors.

1.12   **Waste** – scrap or obsolete stock resulting from the organisation's processes. All organisations produce waste and it often requires storage whilst awaiting disposal. If the waste is toxic or potentially dangerous in any way, special precautions will be needed to render it harmless.

1.13   **Opening stock** – the unit content mentions this as a category of inventory. It just means the stock (of raw materials, work in progress and finished goods) that happens to be on hand when the organisation's accounting period begins. Similarly, **closing stock** is simply the stock of all categories that happens to be on hand when the accounting period ends.

1.14   Some items may fall into different groups but these are the common groups. Remember that one organisation's finished product is another's bought-in part or material. For example, an electrical company producing and packing starter motors or alternators finishes and sells that product to a motor manufacturer. However, to the motor manufacturer, it is only another part in their bill of materials making up the engine unit as a subassembly of their finished product, the vehicle.

Inventory stock management

1.15 Another way of classifying stocks is to focus on their relative importance. At one extreme, some stocks (such as basic stationery items) are relatively unimportant. If the organisation runs short of pencils, for example, it will be very easy to get new stocks in, and there is no danger that business will be disrupted in the meantime.

1.16 At the other extreme, there may be a crucial component absolutely vital to the organisation's production activities and available from only one specialist supplier. The consequences of running out of stock (stocking out, to use the common term) could be very serious. It might take the one supplier weeks to deliver replacement stocks, during which time production activities might be halted.

1.17 The purpose of classifying stocks by their relative importance is so that we know where to direct management attention. Nobody needs to be keeping a close eye on stocks of biros; but the responsible manager must keep a very wary eye on stocks of the critical component.

1.18 Another way of classifying stocks in order of their importance is to calculate the value of different stock items. This is sometimes called **ABC analysis**.

- Items classified as Category A ('the vital few') may be few in number, but require close management attention because of their high monetary value. It would be wasteful of cash to hold excessive stocks of such items, but at the same time it might be disruptive to stock out. A careful balance is required.
- Items classified as Category C ('the trivial many') include the numerous small items that occupy space in most stores areas. Because of their low value it would not make sense to devote a lot of management time to monitoring the stock levels. It is sufficient to set in place a system – invariably nowadays an automated system – to ensure that stocks are regularly replenished.
- Items classified as Category B, naturally, fall between these two extremes and may require a moderate amount of management attention, but not as much as Category A items.

1.19 This process of monitoring stock levels to ensure that neither too much stock is held nor too little – perhaps using techniques such as ABC analysis – is known as **stock management** (or **inventory management**).

2 Reasons for holding stock

Why hold stock at all?

2.1 If you are aware of modern ideas on just in time (JIT) purchasing you may be wondering why organisations need to hold all the categories of stock just described – or why they need to hold stock at all.

2.2 Ideally (for reasons we will see later) a company would work toward holding little or no stock. Many organisations today do indeed aim for a JIT approach to their operations. They take the view that holding stocks is not a good idea.

2.3 Most managers would regard this as a truism and much work is currently being done, by many organisations, to try to reduce stockholding. However, many organisations still hold stocks and some hold large quantities of many items. What, then, are the main reasons for holding stock?

Such reasons exist because of practical considerations relating to the production process and the need to offer high levels of service to customers. We look at these reasons in more detail in the paragraphs that follow.

2.4 Holding stocks can help to minimise production costs. It is expensive to set up machines, and to schedule materials and the workforce. Costs can be minimised by gaining economies of scale in production, but this implies that we accept the need for long production runs, and this in turn implies large stockholdings.

2.5 For an organisation pursuing this policy, the cost of holding stock would be balanced against the costs involved should materials not be available when required. Stock control systems such as materials requirements planning (MRP – which we discuss in a later chapter) work towards forecasting requirements and lead times so as to minimise stockholding and its associated costs.

2.6 Another reason for holding stock is to allow for unpredictable lead times. It takes time to produce items in Stage 1 of a production process, and these will be needed for Stage 2. If we don't have any stock of the Stage 1 items, Stage 2 will be halted, which is expensive and disruptive. At the end of the production process, the consequences are even worse: if we don't have any stock of finished products, we will not be able to meet customer demand and we risk losing business.

2.7 A similar situation arises when there is a disparity between amounts delivered by suppliers and amounts used from day to day. Amounts delivered may be dictated, for example, by a supplier's minimum order quantities. Holding stock allows for a range of goods to be available at short delivery time scales. It all adds up to the convenience of having items available as and when required without making special purchasing arrangements.

2.8 A further reason for holding stock is to take advantage of bulk discounts. There are situations where the value of a bulk discount exceeds the costs of holding large stocks. In such a case, we may place an order for quantities in excess of what we immediately need in order to qualify for the discount. The excess items are held in stock.

2.9 Sometimes we order high quantities to allow for price fluctuations and speculation. Prices, particularly of commodities or semi-manufactured goods, may fluctuate considerably. Some companies may adopt a policy where goods are bought if the price is considered favourable. If this occurs the goods purchased would need to be held in stock until required for use. This depends very much on the goods not being perishable and there being a forecast that they will be used at some point in the future.

2.10 Another reason for holding stock is to accommodate seasonal fluctuations. Supply variations may occur as goods are produced for certain times of the year. For example, toy manufacturers will build up stocks of finished goods in the months leading up to Christmas, so that they can meet expected demand at their peak selling period.

2.11 We may also hold stock to protect against the effects of errors in our forecasts of sales demand, inaccurate records, mistakes in planning and fluctuations in sales or production. Of course, we hope that these errors will not happen but we have to accept that they sometimes do.

2.12 An operational reason for holding stocks is to guard against breakdown or programme changes. Such events can alter the amount of materials that we thought would be needed. Having stock on hand can help to cater for this eventuality.

1

2.13 There is an administrative cost involved in placing orders with suppliers. To minimise this, we may aim to reduce the number of orders we place. By doing so, we accept that the order quantity each time will be greater than it would otherwise be – which means that we will be holding significant amounts in stock, rather than using the materials immediately.

2.14 Some organisations may carry stock as their core activity; for example, a retailer, wholesaler or merchandiser selling stocks directly to their customers. In this business sector, holding large stocks of a wide range of items is seen as being useful in terms of attracting and retaining customers.

2.15 An organisation may hold stock as a support function. For example, a manufacturer might require stocks of maintenance items to keep a production process operating, or a hospital might require stocks of pharmaceuticals to deliver patient care.

2.16 Some items are held in stock simply because they appreciate in value. Examples include wine, timber and spirits.

2.17 Not all of these reasons for holding stock will apply to all organisations but they will all apply, to a greater or lesser extent, to organisations irrespective of type or the sector of the economy in which they operate.

2.18 Some commentators argue that many of these reasons for holding stock are, more correctly, **masking strategies**. They argue that these are not real reasons for holding stock but merely mask problems experienced elsewhere. For example, we mentioned that stocks may be held to cater for unpredictable lead times. The alternative view is that, instead of holding stock to 'mask' this problem, buyers and purchasing staff should work to redress the problem at its root, by improving predictions of lead times.

Summary: reasons for holding stock

2.19 The reasons for holding stock can therefore be summarised as follows.

- Reducing the risk of disruption to production arising from supply shortages or supplier failures
- Reducing the risk of disruption to production from long or uncertain delivery lead times or inaccurate demand forecasting
- Avoiding the risks and costs of stockouts (lost production, lost sales, service failure, damaged customer relations)
- Allowing the rapid replenishment of goods in constant use or demand (eg MRO)
- Enabling fewer, larger orders, which may offer bulk discounts, lower prices and reduced transaction costs
- Enabling stockpiling of goods at best available terms and prices (eg in a market where supply is growing scarce and/or prices are rising)
- Holding almost-finished goods, pre-prepared for late customisation or finishing, to maximise agility, speed and flexibility of response to customer requirements
- Holding finished goods, pre-prepared for anticipated peaks in demand, to smooth out capacity utilisation
- Holding stocks which appreciate in value (eg art works, property or wine).

3   Customer service and availability

Safety stocks

3.1   Rushton, Oxley & Croucher (in *The Handbook of Logistics and Distribution Management*) define safety stock as 'stock that is used to cover the unpredictable daily or weekly fluctuations in demand'. It is sometimes referred to as 'buffer stock'.

3.2   Another way of putting this would be to say that safety stocks are held in order to avoid running out of stock. As we will see, however, it is not *quite* as simple as that.

3.3   Warehouse managers (or whoever is responsible for controlling inventory) have three basic decisions to make regarding stocks of items.

- How frequently they should re-order items
- What quantity of an item should be ordered each time re-ordering takes place
- What quantity of each item should be held in stock

3.4   The first two of the above decisions can be resolved by considering stock replenishment models such as fixed order point or periodic review systems. We look at this in Chapter 4. The question of how much stock to hold involves deciding how much **safety stock** is required.

3.5   There is no 'magic formula' for this but a number of things should be taken into account.

- The item's delivery lead time: this is the supplier's delivery time, plus administrative time for requisitioning, ordering, receipt, inspection distribution and settling any problems which may arise
- The variability in lead times
- The item's demand or usage: consideration should be given to the possibility of quantity discounts when ordering
- The variability of demand or usage
- The desired service level that we want to give users of the item (see below)

3.6   In setting safety stock levels, reasonable assessments of abnormal consumption or usage, and/or delivery delays have to be taken into account. Average usage, average lead time, highest usage and lowest lead time, recorded over any period of time, might be used as a basis for establishing safety stock. However, if lead time is known and constant, the safety stock need only be the quantity of the item that will be used during the lead time period.

3.7   If demand varies greatly it may well be necessary to hold large safety stocks to compensate for extreme variations. The same applies if the supplier's lead time varies greatly. Modern purchasing practice and quality systems would seek to avoid safety stocks as these would be classed as a symptom of a deeper problem. For example, reliance on buffer stocks suggests we cannot rely totally on our supplier to meet our operational needs or we cannot rely on the quality of our forecasting and demand information to cover our needs.

3.8   We can also say that safety stock is related to the accuracy of forecasting, and is in fact a function of the forecast error. If the forecast error is large, the safety stock will also have to be large, while if the error is small, a low safety stock is indicated.

Calculating service levels

3.9 The term 'service level' can have different meanings in different contexts. However, when we are discussing warehousing and the keeping of stock, we can say that service level is the number of occasions, usually expressed as a percentage, when demand is satisfied completely. Demand may be from production departments (who want materials to be used in production), or external customers (who wish to purchase finished products).

3.10 This can be expressed as a formula, as follows:

$$\% \text{ service level} = \frac{\text{Number of times the quantity of the item is supplied}}{\text{Number of times the quantity of the item is requested}} \times 100$$

3.11 Thus, if the item is requested 100 times and is supplied 100 times, the service level is 100%. On the other hand, if it is requested 100 times and supplied 94 times, the service level is 94%. On the other six occasions, presumably, supply was not possible because we did not have sufficient stock.

3.12 An alternative way of expressing this is to say that service level is the complement of the probability of a stockout. Thus, if the probability of a stock out is 4%, the service level is 96%.

3.13 Typically, organisations will strive for a service level of 95% or higher. However, there will be situations in some organisations where a 100% service level would be required. An example would be emergency equipment or drugs in a hospital.

3.14 In order to provide a higher service level, it is necessary to hold higher safety stocks. This, of course, increases the cost of storage and it is sometimes said that, once a service level is above 90%, increasing it by 1% would double storage costs. Certainly, statistical analysis has shown that storage costs will double if the service level is increased from 98% to 99.9%. Figure 1.1 demonstrates this aspect of service level.

Figure 1.1 *The relation between service levels and stockholding costs*

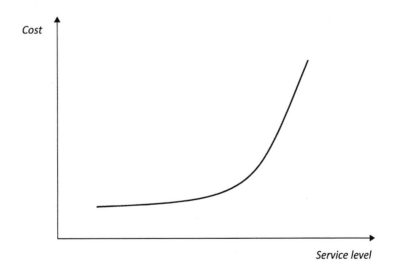

3.15 You should note from the illustration that fairly large increases in service level from a small (poor) level increase costs by very little. However, once the service level has become reasonably high, small increases tend to result in great cost increases.

3.16 We should mention that there is a reverse method of describing this storage cost increase that is commensurate with increasing service levels. This method states that additional increases in inventory (and with them an increase in storage costs) provide progressively smaller increases in service levels. This is sometimes referred to as a diminishing return. Essentially, if the service level is already close to perfect, we can't improve it hugely no matter what resources we devote to the problem.

3.17 Whichever way we prefer expressing this it is certainly true that reducing the amount of safety stock of an item held will reduce the service level related to it.

The service level required: working with sales and marketing

3.18 As we have said, the higher the service level, the higher the cost of storage. This storage cost would, almost certainly, have to be passed on to users or customers. In most cases, users or customers would not expect a 100% service level. Except in cases such as hospitals, as mentioned above, users or customers would prefer a lower service level than a higher one that resulted in paying a higher price due to the cost of the stock required to provide it.

3.19 Providing a service level that satisfies customer requirements requires a clear understanding of those requirements. This suggests working with customers to gain understanding of their requirements. Neither party would gain anything by having service levels that would lead to a long-term loss of profitability for either party.

3.20 It could be argued that the kind of information we have mentioned above regarding service levels is the province of the organisation's marketing or customer relations department, at least in so far as we discuss service to external customers. However, if customers are forewarned of any stockout, they are less likely to be inconvenienced and thus disappointed with our organisation's service. This should mean that the risk of losing the customer diminishes.

3.21 Purchasing and supply staff might need to negotiate internal service levels with users (internal customers). This is because the users may be unaware of the cost of holding stock and may insist on a 100% service level, not realising the cost of this policy.

3.22 Order quantities will depend, to some extent, on safety stock levels but also depend on such matters as the desired maximum stock level and more importantly, the item's lead time and the reliability of the lead time.

Risks and costs of stocking out

3.23 The main risk of being out of stock is that, in many types of organisation, operations would not be able to continue without stocks of necessary materials. The effect of this differs depending on the type of organisation and what it is trying to achieve. In all organisations, however, there is likely to be considerable cost attached to being out of stock.

3.24 In a manufacturing company, the risk is that the production line is likely to stop producing. If this were to continue for any length of time, the company would risk gaining a reputation for poor delivery to its own customers. This would be likely to have the effect of driving customers away, which is something that no company would want.

3.25 In terms of cost, large manufacturers have been known to state that a day's lost production would cost millions. This might be an exaggeration but there would certainly be a heavy cost associated with losing production. This would, of course, include the cost of losing sales to customers but could also include:

- The cost of having to lay workers off on full pay because of the lack of operations continuing (if the company was out of stock for a long time).
- The cost of heating and lighting buildings that would probably need to remain open.

3.26 Public sector organisations would not be able to continue to offer their service if they did not have enough stock of necessary materials and equipment. This would be particularly serious in hospitals because it is possible that certain types of medical care would not be possible until stocks were replenished. Thankfully, this is a rare occurrence.

3.27 In other types of public sector organisation, lack of stock to make emergency repairs could be serious. For example, imagine that one of the water supply companies has a broken water main. If it does not have stock of items to make the repair, there will be flooding in the area and lack of water supply to local residents.

3.28 In the retail sector, if supermarkets lacked stock of some items, it is likely that a customer finding the supermarket to be out of stock and being able to locate the item at a competitor would not return to the first supermarket. In an extremely competitive market this would potentially be quite serious.

3.29 In the 'not-for-profit' sector of the economy it is unlikely that lack of stock would cause major problems. It is worth noting, however, that not having stock of important repair material or equipment would be serious if a building suffered damage and required an emergency repair.

Chapter summary

- There is a wide variety of types of stock including raw materials; consumables; finished stock awaiting sale.
- The type(s) of stock held by organisations usually depends on the nature of the organisation's business or, if in the public sector or not-for-profit sector, its purpose.
- Holding stock is important in many environments despite the fact that just in time (JIT) is becoming increasingly popular.
- There are many reasons for holding stock including the ability to obtain bulk discounts by buying large quantities and holding stock until usage is required.
- The main reason for holding stock is that, in some situations, holding stock can reduce costs. It can also help reduce uncertainty in many situations such as when requirements are not known precisely.
- There is a view that holding stock merely 'masks' problems elsewhere in the organisation. For this reason, some people would prefer the term 'justifications' to be used in connection with stockholding rather than 'reasons'.
- The main problem with not having stock (or running out of stock) in most organisations in most sectors is that lack of stock might prevent performance of operations.
- Lack of operational performance is likely to cost the organisation a lot of money as well as causing bad publicity owing to operations not happening.

Self-test questions

Numbers in brackets refer to the paragraphs above where your answers can be checked.

1 State two types of stock required for producing finished goods on a production line. (1.2–1.4)

2 Why might it be considered important to hold stocks of machine spares? (1.8)

3 Why might an organisation need to hold stocks of waste material? (1.12)

4 What are typical production costs? (2.4)

5 How can holding stock help buyers obtain bulk discounts? (2.8)

6 What kinds of items might be held in stock in order to allow them to appreciate in value? (2.16)

7 List factors relevant to deciding how much safety stock should be held. (3.5)

8 What might be described as the main risk of being out of stock? (3.23)

9 State two costs associated with not being able to continue operations. (3.25)

CHAPTER 2

The Costs of Inventory

Assessment criteria and indicative content

Assess the costs involved in holding inventory

- Acquisition and holding costs
- Methods for the valuation of inventory such as LIFO, FIFO, average cost and standard cost
- The profit and loss entry of cost of sales and goods sold
- The balance sheet entry for inventory

Section headings

1. The valuation of inventory
2. The costs of holding inventory
3. The costs of acquiring inventory

1 The valuation of inventory

The reasons for stock valuation

1.1 All stocks represent capital 'tied up'. This is because the more money we have spent on purchasing or manufacturing stock, the less we have free for other uses. For this reason, organisations usually want to reduce the amount of inventory held and improve stock turnover times. However, it is particularly important to focus on high-value items in order to achieve financial savings. The valuation of stock at the time is one of the ways in which supplies managers may be aware of the extent of capital tied up in inventory.

1.2 In addition to giving supplies managers an ongoing picture of the value of their inventory, and at the same time an indication of the reduction in value (depreciation) suffered by most items held in stock, stock valuation has a number of other purposes. We look at some of these in the paragraphs below.

1.3 **Insurance** – the value of goods held in stock will have a direct bearing on insurance premiums, covering loss or damage. Insurance premiums usually increase as stock value increases and decrease as stock value decreases.

1.4 **General awareness** – the valuation of stock can help create a general awareness of the cost of inventory among all supplies staff. This should encourage efforts to reduce the amount of inventory. It can also allow managers to consider such things as stock levels. In the context of other supplies staff, it can have a bearing on the type of relationship sought with the supplier of each item. Generally, a closer relationship would be sought with suppliers of high-value stock.

1.5 **ABC analysis** – knowing the value of stock items is essential for ABC analysis.

1.6 **Balance sheet and profit and loss account** – valuing stock will assist supplies staff in providing a monetary figure for stock in the financial statements. For most organisations, there is a legal requirement to produce audited financial statements, including a balance sheet and a profit and loss account. The value of an organisation's stock must be included in the balance sheet and profit and loss account.

1.7 **Benchmarking** – knowledge of the value of stock allows benchmarking against other organisations, usually similar in nature, to ascertain whether any efficiency improvements may be achieved.

Calculating the balance sheet entry for inventory

1.8 Valuing stock is not an exact science, and various methods are used in practice, none of which can be regarded as 'correct'. The aim is to calculate an amount which reasonably reflects the stock value.

1.9 The methods specified in your syllabus are cost-based methods. This means that the starting point for the valuation exercise is the suppliers' invoices showing the cost that we paid for the stock items. It is the cost of the organisation's stock at the beginning and end of the accounting period that is shown in the financial statements.

1.10 First, we mention a couple of points relating to terminology. The term **pricing** is often used to describe these methods, even though this term would more usually apply to the selling prices charged by the organisation to its customers (whereas we are really talking about the costs paid to suppliers). And you may meet the term **issue pricing**, meaning the value of the stock at the time it is issued (issued from stores to a production department, or issued from a retail outlet to a paying customer etc).

1.11 It may seem a simple exercise to determine the cost of a stock item. Surely we can just check the supplier's invoice? However, it is not as simple as that if we regularly purchase batches of the stock item. At any point in time, there will be a number of units in stock, and it will not be clear which batch each unit came from. This would not cause a problem if all batches were paid for at the same price, but in practice different batches arrive at different costs.

1.12 In theory, we could somehow attempt to identify which batch each unit came from and build up a cost from there. In practice, this would rarely be possible (and even if it was, the increased accuracy would not justify the time and effort). So instead we adopt a rule of thumb: we assume that items coming into stock are used in a particular order.

1.13 We can assume that items are issued from stock in the same order as they came into stock (first in, first out, or FIFO – ie an issue of units is deemed to have come from the earliest batch received). Or alternatively, we can assume that issues are made from the batches received most recently (last in, first out or LIFO).

1.14 **FIFO** is the more widely practised of the two variations. Each consignment received has its own purchase price and issues are made at the price of the first consignment until that quantity is exhausted. Issues are then made at the price of the second consignment, and so on. This method of stock valuation is illustrated in Table 2.1

Table 2.1 *FIFO stock valuation*

Receipts			Issues			Balance	
Quantity	Cost/unit	Total value	Quantity	Cost/unit	Total value	Quantity	Total value
	$	$		$	$		$
100	25	2,500				100	2,500
100	30	3,000				200	5,500
			40	25	1,000	160	4,500
			60	25	1,500	100	3,000
			20	30	600	80	2,400
400	35	14,000				480	16,400
			80	30	2,400	400	14,000
			40	35	1,400	360	12,600
			240	35	8,400	120	4,200

1.15 Here, we receive two batches of 100 units each, the first costing $25 per unit, the second $30 per unit. When we then issue 40 units to a production department we assume that these came from the first delivery, at $25. The same is true when we subsequently issue another 60 units. At that point, the first batch is exhausted, so that when we then issue another 20 units, they must be deemed to have come from the second batch, at $30. You should be able to work through the rest of Table 2.1 to consolidate your understanding.

1.16 It will be seen that, at any time, the value of the balance remaining is the amount of money which has actually been paid for that amount of stock, at the price of the latest consignments. This facilitates calculation of the value of stocks for balance sheet purposes, because all items are already recorded at cost price. Another advantage of the FIFO method is that, since issues are charged at actual prices, no apparent profits or losses arise as a result of the pricing arrangements.

1.17 There are two common objections to the method.

- It is cumbersome and costly in operation, particularly if there is a lot of movement in purchase prices.
- It does not provide a good basis for comparing job costs, as it is possible for material to be issued at the same time for two jobs, but at different prices.

1.18 The FIFO approach at least enables the balance sheet to give a fair commercial valuation of the stock balance, and is acceptable to the UK tax authorities. (It is worth checking local rules if you are not UK-based.)

1.19 The last in, first out (**LIFO**) method of pricing also uses actual purchase prices as its foundation. However, issues are made at the cost of the most recently received consignment. LIFO is not acceptable to the UK tax authorities as a basis for stock valuation, although it is quite widely practised in some other countries.

1.20 We will not explain the workings of LIFO in detail, but you may like to try applying it to Table 2.1. To get you started, the first issue of 40 units would be priced at $30 per unit, being the cost paid for the batch received most recently.

1.21 You will have noticed that FIFO and LIFO are somewhat cumbersome to use. To avoid this complexity, some organisations use an **average cost** (or AVCO). Variations of this are found in practice, but the usual method is simply to calculate the total number of units on hand and the total amount paid for them. Divide the total cost by the total number of units to obtain the average cost.

1.22 In Table 2.1, if we were using AVCO, we would calculate the average cost per unit after receiving the first two batches as $5,500/200 units, or $27.50 per unit. The first issue of 40 units would then be valued at 40 × $27.50 = $1,100.

1.23 The principal disadvantage of AVCO is the amount of calculating work involved. This may be overcome by the use of electronic systems that handle the arithmetic without difficulty. There are, however, the advantages of minimising the effects of rapid or substantial price changes, and showing the stock remaining at cost price.

1.24 The final method mentioned by your syllabus is **standard cost**. This is a predetermined cost fixed on the basis of up-to-date knowledge of market prices and conditions. It is set for a given period of time, eg six or twelve months, and is kept fixed during that time, irrespective of the actual prices paid for receipts of material. At the end of the fixed period, the standard is reviewed, altered if necessary, and put into operation for a further period.

1.25 As both receipts and issues are valued as standard, there is no real need to show the total values of each transaction on stock records, because the value of stock on hand at any time is easily calculated by multiplying the quantity balance by the standard cost.

1.26 The use of standard costing has significant advantages.

- Clerically, it is easier than any other method.
- By eliminating variations in cost due to price changes, it gives a better indication of efficiency in the use of materials.
- It avoids any delay in obtaining a price and therefore speeds up record keeping and costing operations.

1.27 The only disadvantage is that the organisation's annual published accounts must show actual costs rather than standard costs. There is therefore a year-end exercise to calculate the difference between standard costs and actual costs so that the annual accounts can be adjusted.

Calculating the profit and loss entry for cost of sales

1.28 Any of the methods above can be used to calculate the value of a stock item at a particular moment (say, on the balance sheet date). Once we have performed the exercise for all the different stock lines we hold, we simply aggregate the separate valuations to derive the total stock value. This value appears as an asset in the balance sheet.

1.29 However, stock valuation also impacts on the profit and loss account. This will normally show a value for gross profit, being the value of goods that we have sold to our customers during the year, minus the cost of the goods sold. (Cost of goods sold is often referred to as cost of sales – the two terms are completely equivalent.)

1.30 The cost of goods sold is not simply the amount that our suppliers have invoiced to us in the period (ie our **purchases** for the period), for two reasons.

- Firstly, because this ignores the value of the goods that were already in stock at the beginning of the year (and which were presumably sold during the year). In other words, we have to add to the purchases figure the value of any **opening stock.**
- Secondly, the purchases figure includes the cost of goods that we haven't yet sold in the year because they are still in stock at the end of the year. In other words, we have to deduct from the purchases figure the value of any **closing stock.**

1.31 The profit and loss entry for cost of sales is therefore calculated by means of the following formula.

Cost of sales = opening stock + purchases – closing stock

2   The costs of holding inventory

Damage

2.1 The decision to hold stocks is not straightforward, because there are problems and costs associated with stockholding. The costs are normally classified as holding costs – the costs we incur by holding stocks in a warehouse, store room or similar – and acquisition costs – the costs we incur by the very process of ordering stocks and bringing them to our premises. In this section we look at holding costs; in the following section of the chapter we look at acquisition costs. Our first category of holding cost is the cost of damage to stocks.

2.2 If items in stock are handled carelessly, they might become damaged. Clearly, this is most likely to be the case with fragile items such as those made of glass. However, even sturdier items such as those made of steel could become bent if dropped. Also, apparently sturdy material such as concrete blocks could become chipped if knocked over.

2.3 Such damage might cause the items to be useless. This means that they would need to be replaced at extra cost to the organisation. In this situation they would need to be 'written off', meaning that the money spent on them was wasted. Additionally, the money spent on the items could not be recovered by selling them to other users. Some of their value might be recovered by selling them for scrap but this, of course, would only recoup a fraction of their original value. Insurance could mitigate this problem – we discuss this possibility later in the chapter.

2.4 The occurrence of damaged stock can be reduced as follows.

- Check stock carefully as it is received into stores. Damaged or inadequate packaging needs action to ensure that the stock will be protected.
- Use stock in the order in which it is received.
- Maintain conditions that are appropriate to the type of stock – for example, in terms of temperature, humidity and so on.
- Train all staff in the use of handling equipment and stress the importance of moving stock items carefully.

Deterioration

2.5 This has a similar effect on the cost of storage but is different in nature. Deterioration happens to some types of items or material if they are kept in stock for a long time. Examples include the following (there are many other possibilities).

- Paper can become discoloured.
- Iron and steel items can become rusty.
- Damp could cause cement to become solid and therefore unusable.

2.6 As with damage, deterioration will increase the cost of storage because it means that items affected will be useless. As with damaged items, items that have deteriorated will incur costs of replacement. Once again, they may be able to be sold for scrap, which would mitigate such costs. Insurance, also, would help mitigate such losses.

2.7   The likelihood of deterioration could be minimised by reducing stockholding. More effective, however, would be to ensure that goods likely to deteriorate are stored in suitable conditions. An example would be keeping materials that are susceptible to damp in dry locations.

Loss of value

2.8   This can happen in two ways: through obsolescence or redundancy.

2.9   **Obsolescence** is usually due to items being held in stock for long periods of time. During this time advancing technology makes the items outdated. In a retail organisation, customers would no longer want to purchase such items. In other types of organisation, it would almost certainly mean that the person(s) who had requested the item would no longer want it.

2.10   Costs lost through obsolescence might be mitigated by selling the item secondhand. A better approach would be to reduce the possibility of it occurring by accurately forecasting usage. Then items could be purchased and held in stock in small quantities and only replenished when those in stock had been used.

2.11   **Redundancy** occurs when items are held in stock for a long time and there comes a point where they are no longer required. Such a situation usually originates from purchasing the item in too large a quantity to start with. In retail organisations, particularly those selling items that are subject to fashion, redundancy might occur because of changes in consumers' tastes.

2.12   Redundant items would need to be sold secondhand or for scrap, once again meaning a loss of value. The best way of mitigating the effects of redundancy would be to forecast requirements as accurately as possible. Again, you could add to this the idea of purchasing the item in small quantities frequently rather than a large quantity at one time. Any loss of bulk discount occurring because of this would probably be outweighed by the fact that the items do not become redundant. It might also be possible, if forecasting can be accurate, to negotiate a discount based on annual consumption whilst scheduling small, frequent, deliveries.

Fraud

2.13   Fraud may arise because a member of staff is seeking to achieve an illicit personal gain. It might also occur where staff are trying to mask inefficiencies such as losses of stock items.

2.14   Here are some typical warehouse frauds arising from criminal activity.

- Claiming that materials have been delivered short by the supplier – when in fact the consignment was delivered fully and correctly.
- Claiming that materials were received as damaged or faulty from the supplier – when in fact the consignment was delivered in good condition.
- Over-picking an order so that surplus materials are on the warehouse floor – ready to be picked up and taken away.
- Putting extra materials on to a delivery vehicle for an unauthorised delivery.
- Plain petty theft.
- Failing to book in certain attractive stock returns (items returned by users or customers because they are not needed) and stealing the materials.

2.15   Fraud carried out to mask losses or inefficiencies might include over-valuing stocks or materials in order to hide losses incurred elsewhere.

2.16 We need to eradicate or, at least, minimise fraud. Documentation for issue should be required for any materials to be issued out of the warehouse area. Issuing materials without the correct documentation will lead to stock losses and create a possibility of fraudulent practices. Nowadays, issuing stocks without any documentation is only likely to occur within very small warehousing functions or privately owned businesses.

2.17 The documents warehouses require to issue materials may be computer generated and highly detailed with barcodes etc, or may just be a basic record of the quantity that has been issued out and to whom. The key requirement of the documentation is that it creates an 'audit trail'. In other words, if there is a discrepancy between the book stock and the physical stock, documentation is in place to trace where the error has occurred. ('Book stock' means the amount of stock indicated by the company's records; it may differ from 'physical stock', which is the amount of stock actually present.)

2.18 Traditionally signatures are required to issue goods out, but with modern technology individuals may possess barcode identification. If the record is 'swiped' with a 'wand' or 'reader' then you are registered as the stock issuer. Users of stock items or customers may be provided with PIN numbers or passwords to allow them to receive items legitimately.

Cost of storage

2.19 The costs of storing stock can be quite considerable. Here are some of the major cost elements.

- Interest on the value of stores in stock (ie loss of interest on capital tied up in this way). This is sometimes referred to as an opportunity cost: we forgo the opportunity to invest cash, eg in a bank deposit account, and instead use it to pay for stock. The opportunity cost is the amount of bank interest we forgo.
- The operating expenses of storehouses, including wages, depreciation of equipment, rent and rates, repairs, heating and lighting, maintenance of buildings and machinery, and the costs of vehicles and handling equipment, including their running and maintenance costs.
- Loss, deterioration and obsolescence of stock.
- Insurance, stock checking, recording and accounting. We will look at these costs in more detail later.

2.20 The cost of holding any particular item of stock is a somewhat elusive problem. It is first necessary to decide what factors are to be included in the cost – these have been outlined above. After that, it is common to express the cost of holding an item in stock for a year as a percentage of the item's cost. But this too causes difficulties: the true cost of storing a bag of cement may be very similar to storing a similar volume of a precious metal, but clearly the 'percentage' method will lead to very different results in these two cases.

2.21 Another point is that temporary fluctuations in the levels of stocks within reasonable limits do not substantially affect some of the factors such as depreciation of buildings, rates, repairs and wages. The warehouses will not be extended or curtailed in size and the staff will not be increased or reduced in number because of minor changes in the amount of stock on hand.

2.22 Despite all these difficulties, it is possible to arrive at the total cost of holding stock for a given period of time (say one year) and, by relating that total sum of money to the average value of stock held during the period, to calculate the average cost of holding stock as a percentage of the value of the goods themselves. The figure can then be regarded as the nominal cost of storage for any given item, and is often in the range of 20–30% of the item's cost.

2.23 It is common, in most organisations, to set an annual budget for the above costs and to monitor progress on a monthly basis by comparing actual costs against budgeted costs.

Cost of security

2.24 In some warehouses, this can be a perennial problem. Some warehouses store a great many valuable and 'attractive' items. If they are stolen in significant quantities, the company will lose a large amount of value each year, thus greatly increasing the cost of storage. Other warehouses may not carry such valuable items but may suffer from internal pilferage of such things as small tools.

2.25 As a general rule, if people want to get hold of the items you carry in your warehouse badly enough, they will find a way of doing so. This is particularly true of 'attractive' items. These are usually items that would be useful at home or which could be sold on at a good price. Warehouse managers must do everything possible to keep such theft and pilferage to a minimum.

2.26 Here are some specific measures that may be taken to reduce or eliminate theft and pilferage.

- Limit access to staff so that only stores personnel are allowed to enter the warehouse. This will minimise, if not eliminate, pilferage of stock items.
- Keep buildings locked when not in use and consider employing a watchman or security staff. Remember that outside security companies can provide various levels of service for out-of-hours surveillance. Such a service would incur a cost but this could well be outweighed by reducing or eliminating stock losses.
- All goods received should be checked accurately for quantity, weight, specification etc. Remember that, if you do not know what has arrived, it is unlikely that you will know if items are going missing.
- Adequate systems of stock-checking and auditing should be implemented (see later in the course). These measures keep a constant check on what you have and should inform you of anything going missing. Knowledge of what items are going missing helps you to take steps elsewhere to prevent it.
- Correctly authorised issues – items should only be issued against a properly signed and authorised requisition.
- Adequate records to be maintained – if you do not know what you have and keep a record of what comes in and what goes out, you will not know if anything is going missing.
- Delivery drivers confined to Goods Receiving bay – limiting the number of people allowed access to the warehouse helps to narrow down the list of possible suspects if pilferage does occur.
- Co-operate with Crime Prevention Officer (CPO) on modern security methods etc. The CPO can advise on, for example, weak points of the building, and on modern security systems.
- Designated key-holders for 24-hour issues. If out-of-hours issues are required it is best to ensure that a responsible person, such as the night shift supervisor, takes charge of it.
- Valuable and attractive items should be segregated. It makes sense to keep items deemed particularly prone to theft in a lockable cupboard or cage.
- Staff should be aware that, if they are caught pilfering, the penalty is likely to be instant dismissal and prosecution. This might seem a hard line but a strong message must be sent out, particularly where pilferage is rife.
- Scrap and items for disposal should be segregated and kept securely. You should remember that such materials, particularly those that will command a good scrap value, are likely to be attractive.

Cost of insurance

2.27 Stock should be insured against the risks of fire, theft or damage (all occurrences that may happen). The value of goods held in stock will have direct bearing on insurance premiums, covering loss or damage, for the warehouse. Insurance premiums usually increase as stock value increases and decrease as stock value decreases.

Cost of depreciation

2.28 Many items that are held in stock for any length of time will depreciate in value. In other words, their value will diminish because they will be perceived as being 'old'. This would apply particularly to retail items. An example might be where supermarkets sell items that are approaching their 'sell by' date below their normal retail price. Depreciation applies to all stock items, however, and is one reason why it is not considered a good idea to hold larger quantities of stock than are necessary.

Opportunity cost of stockholding

2.29 We have already mentioned the concept of opportunity cost. The amount of money we spend on stock reduces the amount we have available for other profitable uses. If we had less stock, we would have more cash available. As a minimum, we could invest such cash in a bank deposit account to earn interest. Alternatively, we could invest it in other profitable trading activities. Either way, the fact that we have used cash to purchase or manufacture stock means that we lose out on the value of that cash in other ways. This is the meaning of opportunity cost.

2.30 There may also be a cost of borrowing money. This will happen if we have to borrow finance in order to pay for items that will be held in stock; we will have to pay interest on the loan. This would add to the opportunity cost of storage and hence to the total stockholding cost.

2.31 These two aspects of financial stockholding costs are reasons why it is always best to keep stockholding to a minimum. Clearly, however, this does not mean that we should reduce stockholding to a level that would damage our operations. A degree of balance is required.

Overheads and use of space

2.32 Essentially, 'overheads' is the term used to describe the fixed costs of running the organisation's stores operation. These will include:

- Rent and rates of the building (and any local taxes)
- Heating and lighting of the building
- Insurance of the buildings against (for example) fire.
- Staff costs
- Storage and handling equipment (some modern types of racking and handling equipment such as forklift trucks can be very expensive).

2.33 The larger the building and the more stock held in it, the greater will be these overhead costs. A large building will almost certainly have greater rental costs. It will require more staff to operate it and will require more energy to heat and light it as necessary. Large premises will also cost more to insure than would smaller premises. (We are referring here to insurance of the building rather than the insurance of stocks that we mentioned above.)

2.34 This brings us to **use of space**. The greater the quantity of stock held, the more space will be required in the stores building. Once again, if we can reduce the amount of stock held to a reasonable minimum, we can reduce the size of the warehouse.

2.35 Thus, use of space is a measure of stores efficiency. If a warehouse is largely empty, the cost of rent and rates, the cost of heating, lighting and power and other costs such as labour and the cost of storage and handling equipment are wasted and are nothing more than a drain on company finances. It is important, therefore, to ensure that the warehouse is as full as it needs to be to provide the organisation's required service level.

2.36 This is not to suggest that the warehouse should be filled simply to achieve this target. If the warehouse is too large, then it is wasting money for reasons just mentioned and thought should be given to 'hiving off' some of it for other purposes or, in extreme cases, renting some of it to outside organisations for temporary storage accommodation.

2.37 If we are in a position to plan a new warehouse building, we should plan it with anticipated demand in mind for as long a period of time into the future as possible. This should ensure that the warehouse is not too large for foreseeable requirements.

3   The costs of acquiring inventory

3.1 When an order is placed, the buying organisation incurs a cost known as the 'ordering cost'. This varies from organisation to organisation but can often be a significant part of the cost of inventory. The cost typically comprises the following elements.

- 'Executive effort': this is the cost of supplier selection
- The cost of tendering, where used
- The cost of stationery and the cost of telephone calls and email usage
- The cost of staff time to process the order
- The cost of receiving goods
- The cost of processing invoices

3.2 This means that the greater the number of orders placed, the higher will be the cost of ordering. Even if one order is placed to cover 12 months' supply (a 'call-off' order or similar), there will still be associated costs such as receiving costs and the costs of verifying and paying invoices.

3.3 However, if a small number of orders is placed for large quantities of an item, the cost of ordering is low. So one way of reducing the costs of ordering would be to place one order for a large quantity of an item (say 12 months worth of usage) and hold the items in stock. The problem with this is that, as we have already seen, holding stock has costs associated with it.

3.4 **Order costs may vary between organisations**, because of a number of factors.

- The efficiency and effectiveness of the order and invoice processing staff and systems used by the organisation – and the rates of pay of staff
- The methods used to place and process orders (eg email, phone, formal tendering process, executive involvement in supplier selection)
- The transaction charges (if any) imposed by suppliers (eg small order surcharges), banks (for handling payments) and so on
- The 'mix' of small and frequent versus large and infrequent orders placed by the organisation,

depending on its approach to inventory management and purchasing (eg whether it uses EOQ, whether it uses call-off contracts)

- The methods used to calculate ordering costs – and so on.

3.5 In summary, there are significant costs incurred in both acquiring and holding stock.

- **Acquisition costs** are incurred when orders are placed: costs of management time, administration, paperwork and transaction charges.
- **Holding costs** include the cost of working capital tied up in stock; the costs of storage; and the costs of damage, deterioration, pilferage and obsolescence while goods are being held.

3.6 The task of the purchasing manager is, ideally, to reduce these costs – but note that there is an inherent trade-off between them.

- You could seek to minimise acquisition costs by making fewer, larger orders – but this would increase your stock levels, and hence your holding costs.
- You could seek to minimise your holding costs by only purchasing stock in small quantities, as and when you need them – but this would increase the frequency of your orders, and hence your acquisition costs.

3.7 How is this dilemma resolved? There will be a certain order quantity at which holding costs will equal acquisition costs – and the total cost will be as low as possible. This is called the economic order quantity or EOQ. We look at the EOQ model in a later chapter.

Chapter summary

- To calculate the value of items held in stock we use a 'rule of thumb'. There are several possibilities: FIFO, LIFO, AVCO and standard costs among them.
- The profit and loss figure for cost of goods sold is calculated as opening stock + purchases – closing stock.
- The value of stocks may be reduced by damage and deterioration and steps should be taken to minimise these.
- Similarly, the value of stocks may be reduced by obsolescence and redundancy and steps should be taken to minimise these.
- The main methods of reducing stockholding to minimise these losses is to forecast usage accurately and reduce the extent of stockholding by (for example) purchasing items in small quantities frequently.
- Theft and pilferage can also add to financial losses which can increase the cost of storage. These can be reduced by having efficient and effective systems such as the recording of stocks moving in and out of the warehouse.
- There are many costs associated with holding stock. These include interest on the value of stores in stock; operating costs of the warehouse; and costs occasioned by losses such as deterioration and damage of items held in stock.
- The total cost of storage is typically between 20% and 30% of the value of the item if it is held in stock for one year.
- Security is very important in a warehouse because losses due to theft and pilferage can be high.
- Opportunity costs relate to other things on which we could have spent the money tied up in stocks. These costs are such things as investment to earn interest or investment in other projects.
- Stockholding can also have negative impact on working capital and cashflow. This is because of money being 'tied up' in stockholding.
- An important aspect of the total cost of storage is the cost of overheads. These are the costs of operating the warehouse and include such things as rent and rates, staffing costs, heating and lighting and the cost of storage and handling equipment.
- The costs of acquiring inventory are high if we have a policy of frequent small orders.

Self-test questions

Numbers in brackets refer to the paragraphs above where your answers can be checked.

1   Explain the use of (a) FIFO and (b) LIFO in the valuation of stock items. (1.14, 1.19)

2   How is the profit and loss figure for cost of goods sold calculated? (1.31)

3   Explain the consequences of stock items becoming damaged. (2.2, 2.3)

4   Explain why stock items might become obsolete. (2.9)

5   Identify the best ways of mitigating the effects of redundancy of stock items. (2.12)

2

6   Identify three types of possible warehouse fraud. (2.14)

7   Describe a typical process of documentation that might be used to allow stock to be issued to users or customers. (2.16, 2.17)

8   Identify four types of warehouse operating costs. (2.19)

9   Describe two measures that may be used to limit stock losses due to theft or pilferage. (2.26)

10   Describe what is meant by opportunity cost. (2.29)

11   Identify three types of stores overhead. (2.32)

12   List elements typically included in the costs of acquiring inventory. (3.1)

CHAPTER 3

Monitoring and Control of Inventory

Assessment criteria and indicative content

 1.3 Explain the main techniques for the monitoring and control of inventory

- Pareto analysis and ABC classifications of inventory
- Dependent and independent demand
- MRP and MRPII
- Just in time supply and *kanban* systems
- Consignment stocking and vendor managed inventory

Section headings

1. Pareto analysis and ABC classification of inventory
2. Dependent and independent demand
3. MRP and MRPII
4. Just in time supply and *kanban* systems
5. Consignment stocking and VMI

1   Pareto analysis and ABC classification of inventory

Pareto analysis

1.1 A large part of the reason for trying to minimise stocks as much as possible is due, as we have seen, to the cost of storage. However, owing to the **opportunity cost** of storage, we need to be much more careful with high-value stocks than with low-value items. One of the best ways of achieving this is to use Pareto analysis. As we will see, this can be used to combine value and usage. These factors interact.

1.2 Within any stores operation there will be a wide variety of materials needed for different purposes. Some items might have a very high usage rate, so if they ran out many customers would be disappointed. Other items might be of particularly high value, and so excessively high inventory levels would be very expensive for the organisation. At the same time, mid-range-value items may have a high usage so the overall spend there may exceed the annual outlay on high-value items.

1.3 Pareto analysis is a means of ranking stock items by their **usage value** (their usage rate multiplied by their individual value). Items with a high usage value require careful control, whereas those with a low usage value need not be controlled so rigorously.

1.4   Generally, a small proportion of the total items contained within an inventory will account for a large proportion of the total usage value. This is known as the **Pareto Law or 80/20 rule**.

1.5   The technique takes its name from Vilfredo Pareto (1848–1923), an Italian economist and sociologist who made the observation that a large proportion of national wealth tended to be under the control of a relatively small number of individuals. This observation enabled him to formulate the following rule: '… in any series of elements to be controlled a selected small factor in terms of number of elements almost always accounts for a large factor in terms of effort'. This rule has been evidenced and applied successfully in numerous business situations.

ABC analysis

1.6   ABC analysis is a refinement of the idea, developing it one stage further into three stock categories that are widely employed. ABC analysis uses the Pareto relationship to classify the different types of items. This allows inventory managers to concentrate their efforts on controlling the most significant items of stock.

- Category A items (high usage value) – typically, these account for the first 20% of items and 80% of usage value. These items require tight control including accurate records, regular review of stock levels and demand forecasts, and close follow-up and expediting to reduce lead time. The traditional view was that these items should be 'turned over' approximately 12 times per annum (ie roughly once a month) but, in today's world of JIT, more frequent turnover would be desired by most managers.
- Category B items (medium usage value) – typically, these account for 10% of items and 10% of usage value. These items need less attention than Category A but still require regular control techniques to be applied.
- Category C items (low usage value) – typically, these account for 70% of items and 10% of usage value. These items do not require close control because their low value does not warrant it. Most companies would keep these items in large quantities (they are usually small in size and will not take up much room in the warehouse) and look to 'turn them over' once or twice per annum.

1.7   ABC analysis measures the relationship between the annual usage value of an individual item and total stock value so that a Category A item is only Category A if its annual usage value is within the top 80% of total annual inventory value. If you think about a warehouse that you are familiar with, there will be a relatively small number of expensive items (Category A) and a large number of inexpensive items (Category C).

1.8   The procedure for sorting items into categories commences by tabulating stock items in a list by part number. Alongside each part number the unit cost and annual usage rate is then entered. The latter two are then multiplied in order to record the annual usage value.

1.9   The next step is to re-list all the items in order of annual usage value starting with the highest, then to record alongside each the cumulative annual usage value and finally each individual percentage of the total.

- **Stage 1: Calculate the annual usage value**

A	B	C	D
			Annual usage
Part number	Unit value	Annual usage	value (B × C)
	$	Units	$
300–171	58.00	6,000	348,000
310–060	6.00	10,000	60,000
691–020	220.00	500	110,000
			518,000

- **Stage 2: Rank the items in descending order of annual usage value**

A	B	C	D	E	F
					D as % of
			Annual	Cum annual	total usage
	Unit value	Annual usage	usage value	usage value	value
	$	Units	$	$	%
300–171	58.00	6,000	348,000	348,000	67
691–020	220.00	500	110,000	458,000	21
310–060	6.00	10,000	60,000	518,000	12

1.10 Clearly any stocklist will have many more items than this simple example, but this is sufficient to illustrate the approach. A typical Pareto distribution is now shown graphically in Figure 3.1.

Figure 3.1 *Pareto analysis*

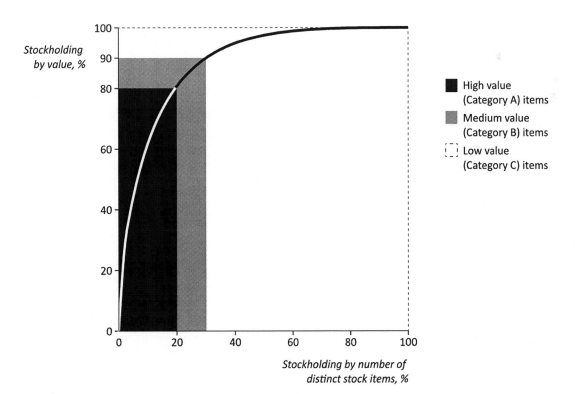

1.11 You should be aware that 'stock turnover' is the term applied to the frequency with which stocks are ordered, used and then re-ordered. This means that if our order quantity is sufficient for one month's usage our stock of that item will turn over 12 times per year. This stock would then be used during the month and steps would be taken to purchase another month's worth of stock for delivery at the end of the month. The smoothness which this system operates would depend greatly on how steady the usage is and on the predictability of the item's lead time.

1.12 As we have already mentioned, we need to pay more attention to the control of high-value items than to low-value ones. The question then arises as to what exactly is high and low value. This might seem fairly obvious but an item that is considered high value in one organisation may be considered low value in another and *vice versa*. Therefore, we need a method of identifying the relative value of items held in stock. This is to allow us to concentrate our efforts on high-value stock to ensure that stock levels are kept to a minimum and stock turnover maximised.

1.13 Efficient management of stocks can have a significant impact upon the profitability of an organisation. For example, a primary responsibility for retailers is to ensure the effective purchase, distribution and arrival of the stock that it will then sell on to its customers. Even a small grocery shop can have a throughput of stock of considerable monetary value.

1.14 The role of stock in manufacturing is also very important. For example, in the electronics industry 75 per cent of operating costs can be in the form of bought-in parts. It is a well known fact that this proportion of bought-in parts has increased markedly in recent decades.

1.15 ABC analysis only takes account of capital tied up in inventory. It has no bearing whatever on the risks or consequences of not having stock when required ('stockouts'). It also ignores supply risk and criticality of items.

1.16 In practical terms, Category A items are those which are regularly used and have a comparatively high unit value. Category B items are either those that are regularly used and have a medium unit value, or those that have a high value but less usage. Category C items are those that are either very rarely used and have low value, or exceptionally low-value items such as fasteners.

1.17 The ABC system is useful because it tells inventory managers where to devote their energy when managing inventory-related costs. Obviously, time spent controlling Category A stock levels is much more rewarding than time spent on Category C items. Usually, re-order quantities and buffer stocks of Category A items would be carefully and regularly reviewed, whereas Category C items will often be managed on a simple two-bin re-order system.

1.18 Table 3.1 gives a brief overview of how we should manage each of the ABC categories of stock item.

Table 3.1 *Managing ABC stock*

CLASS	HOW TO MANAGE THEM
A	Very tight control Order only calculated or known requirements Accurate recording of receipts and issues Schedules constantly reviewed Continuous progressing Minimal buffer stocks (probably less than two weeks)
B	Moderate level of control Order against forecast from historical data Recording of all receipts and issues Moderate level of review of schedules Progress items in short supply or late Larger buffer stocks – say 6–8 weeks
C	Lower level of control Minimal recording of receipts and issues Low level of schedule review No progressing Large safety stocks – say 12 weeks

Other methods of categorising stock

1.19   ABC analysis, based on usage value, is not the only form of differential stock control. Here are some other criteria by which a firm might choose to categorise its stock items.

- The consequences of a stockout situation, with certain items monitored more closely (irrespective of their usage value) because the consequences of a stockout would be serious
- The difficulty or complexity of holding the stock item – size, perishability, and hazardous nature

1.20   The aim is always the same – hold the minimum stock possible to meet customer service criteria.

2   Dependent and independent demand

Defining dependent and independent demand

2.1   Some stock items are subject to dependent demand, while for other items demand is independent. The distinction is important because different systems of stock control apply to the two categories. In the next chapter we will describe stock control systems that apply mainly in situations of independent demand. Where demand is dependent, more sophisticated systems are required (eg materials requirements planning or MRP, discussed later in this chapter).

2.2   **Independent demand** is the easier of the two to understand so we will explain this one first. An item has independent demand characteristics if its demand is **not dependent** on the demand for anything else. The majority of items have independent demand. For example, the demand for desks in an office is not dependent on the demand for anything else. The demand for lubricants in a factory is not dependent on the demand for anything else, and so on. Many consumables and MRO items (maintenance, repair and operating items) are subject to independent demand.

2.3   **Dependent demand** is usually encountered in manufacturing organisations. If we take cars as an example, the demand for engines will be dependent on the demand for cars. We can then add that the demand for gear boxes will be dependent on the demand for engines. Demand for the various cogs that go into a gearbox will be dependent on the demand for gearboxes and so on. Ultimately, demand for each component depends upon the demand for the finished product.

2.4   In non-manufacturing environments it is difficult to identify examples of dependent demand. We could, however, say that demand for ink would depend on demand for pens. Equally, demand for plastic utensils might be dependent on the demand for takeaway cooked food.

Inventory control systems for dependent demand

2.5   Inventory control (or 'stock control': the terms are interchangeable) is the process of ensuring that we have enough (but not too much) stock of an item. It concerns re-ordering stock when necessary so as to ensure that we continue to have enough stock. It also concerns ensuring that we do not run out of stock (a stockout).

2.6   All the systems that carry out this function involve monitoring stock usage and taking the necessary action to re-order as well as being aware of situations when we have too much stock of an item. Again, this last function involves monitoring stock usage.

2.7   Stock control systems designed for items of independent demand do not work well with dependent demand items. In fact, it is often said that the failure of these systems to deal with dependent demand items is their main weakness. They also tend to assume that usage of items is smooth and constant. On production lines, however, demand often occurs at different times and in increments of varying size (a phenomenon known as 'lumpy' demand).

2.8   Before we consider how to control inventory of dependent demand items, we need to look at the nature of production lines. The first concept to consider is the **hierarchy of components**. If you do not have experience of working in a manufacturing environment you may find this concept rather difficult to grasp. The example shown below (Figure 3.2), based on car production, should help.

Figure 3.2 *The hierarchy of components in car manufacture*

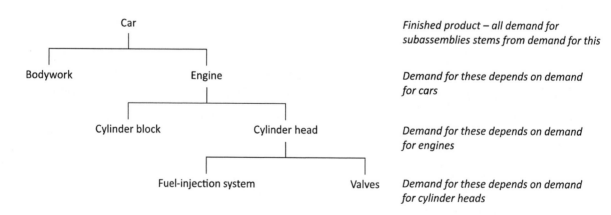

3   MRP and MRPII

Materials requirements planning

3.1   The next problem is how to control inventory of dependent demand items if traditional systems do not really work. In recent decades much work has been done in developing more sophisticated systems to cope with this situation. The most commonly used system is materials requirements planning (MRP). This is invariably an IT-based system that helps determine when items are required for a production line and in what quantities. It can operate manually but this is very rare and would really only work for finished goods containing few components.

3.2   MRP is based on a **master production schedule (MPS)**. This is derived from the company's sales forecast, updated with the latest actual sales information. This provides an estimate of orders that will need to be satisfied during the time period under consideration. Typically, this period would be the next 12 months for a 'mass production' company (a car manufacturer being a good example).

3.3   To the sales forecast would be added actual customer orders, and the company's production policy would also be taken into consideration. The production policy covers matters such as whether the company produces on a 'batch' basis or is a 'jobbing' concern. It would also cover such aspects as whether we will produce Product A (for example) for the next two months or whether it will be Product B and so on. It is likely that a 'batch' producer would have a policy of producing one product for, say, the next month. It would then change its production process to produce another of its product range for, say, two months.

3.4   To give an example of this, consider a hypothetical manufacturer of forklift trucks with two production lines. In Month 1, the first production line is devoted to producing 1,000kg capacity electric pallet trucks, while the second production line is producing 2,000kg capacity diesel forklift trucks. The tooling and equipment is then changed on both lines. During Month 2, the first line produces 1,500kg capacity 'rider' pallet trucks while the second line produces 1,000 kg capacity 'reach' trucks. The types of truck produced, the quantities and the timings would all be dictated by customer orders and sales forecasts.

3.5   Once the MPS has been produced, the next stage is to 'explode' it. This means that the computer software calculates how many of each component is required in order to manufacture the finished products specified in the MPS. The document that results from this process is known as a **bill of materials** (BOM).

3.6   We can illustrate this by reference to our fictional forklift manufacturer. Suppose the MPS shows that 200 1,000kg capacity trucks are to be produced. The BOM will show that 800 wheels are required (four per truck), meaning 4,000 wheel nuts (five per wheel) and so on. The BOM will follow this process for every component and subassembly in the entire truck. This is illustrated in Figure 3.3

Figure 3.3 *Exploding the MPS into the BOM*

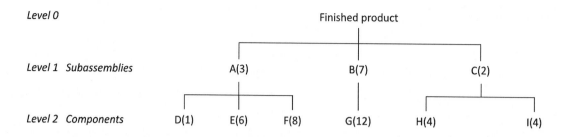

3.7 The MPS and BOM can be converted into an MRP system by adding the following information into the system's database.

- The inventory status file: this tells us which of the required items we already have in stock and in what quantities
- The delivery lead times for all of the items required
- All of these pieces of information should tell us **what** we need to order, in what **quantities** and **when** we need to place the orders. This should then ensure that the right quantities of the right items are delivered to us not too long before being required by the production line. This is not quite just in time production but it is moving in that direction.
- With items being used regularly, it is not uncommon to place them on call-off orders or to use consignment stocking. This is particularly true of items with short lead times and which are readily available.

3.8 In summary, the MRP process is as follows.

- Obtain updated sales forecast – updated with latest *actual* sales information.
- Use sales forecast, customer orders and production policy to form master production schedule (MPS).
- Use MRP software to compute material requirements by 'exploding' end product requirements into successively lower levels in the product structure. This gives the gross requirement for each material and component.
- Use the inventory status file to determine materials and components already in stock. Deduct this from the **gross requirement** to arrive at the **net requirement** for each material and component (ie the quantities we need to order from suppliers).
- Assess the net requirement in the light of supplier lead times in order to determine the schedule for ordering materials and components.
- Place orders with suppliers via the purchasing function
- Receive goods and issue them to the production line.

3.9 This is illustrated in Figure 3.4.

Figure 3.4 *The MRP process*

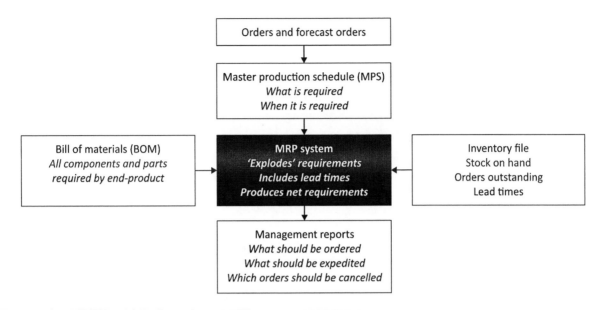

Characteristics of MRP

3.10 There are certain **prerequisites** for using MRP.

- There must be a master production schedule exploded into a bill of materials.
- All inventory items must be identified.
- The bill of materials must exist at planning stage.
- The inventory status of all items is needed.
- File data must have integrity.
- Lead times for each material and component must be known and updated on an ongoing basis.
- All of the quantity relationships to end products must be known (eg how many wheels to a truck; how many wheel nuts to a wheel, etc).
- There must be reliable, flexible suppliers who are committed to supplying against MRP schedules and who will make the system work.

3.11 The advantages of MRP are as follows.

- It reduces inventory.
- It is sensitive to change. Data can be updated as frequently as is necessary.
- It provides a look into the future by forecasting what products are to be produced and what materials will be needed to produce them.
- Inventory control is action-oriented rather than clerically-oriented.
- Order quantities are related to requirements. This is one of the main reasons why MRP reduces inventory.
- MRP reduces 'routine time' in the purchasing job. This is particularly true if requirements are known for a relatively long period of time and remain steady during that time.
- It integrates the thinking and action of personnel in purchasing, production and marketing. This is because it requires information from all three departments as we have seen above.

3.12   The limitations (not necessarily disadvantages) of MRP are as follows.

- It only applies to 'dependent' demand items.
- Its payback on low-value items (Category C items: see earlier in this chapter) may be doubtful. This is because it might be advantageous just to keep fairly large quantities of these items in stock. This would mean that the items would be available when required without costing too much to hold in stock. This would mean that they would also only need to be ordered infrequently, so that the cost of ordering would be low.
- It depends on an accurate forecast which is not always possible.
- It does not apply to many 'jobbing' manufacturers who must keep raw materials on hand to meet what amounts to emergency production orders.

3.13   In conclusion, you should be aware that some organisations may face a number of different types of demand at the same time and may, therefore, need to use a combination of systems to cope with this situation. For example, in a car production plant, production line requirements will exhibit dependent demand characteristics and will be catered for by an MRP system (or similar). The plant's maintenance items will exhibit independent demand characteristics and will be catered for by fixed order point or periodic review systems (see next chapter).

Manufacturing resources planning (MRPII)

3.14   The disciplined approach introduced by MRP has been further developed over the years. Manufacturing resources planning (MRPII) builds on key areas of MRP by considering all the resources needed for production, not just materials. For example, it deals with manpower, machinery and money.

3.15   The differences are made clear in their respective names. Materials requirements planning concentrates on securing the right materials to enable the production run to go ahead. Manufacturing resources planning examines the manufacturing resources required for the production to go ahead, eg the labour costs involved, the costs of machinery and proportion of overheads attributable etc. MRPII enables materials and work to be costed accurately.

3.16   MRPII is a method for planning manufacture and assessing the costs involved. It draws on the aggregate plans via the MPS not only to develop the areas covered by an MRP system but also to allow for such areas as personnel deployment, maintenance planning, and financial analysis.

3.17   Building on the discipline required for traditional MRP systems the MRPII model has led some to say that MRPII adds the financial function to MRP.

3.18   Managers can determine the dates when suppliers must be paid by studying MRP timing of purchase orders and their due dates. Accurate costing of manufacturing can be obtained as the system can look at machines and personnel used and analyse the information to provide accurate costings on production runs. The analysis can be further used as a benchmark for future production runs in order to seek operational improvements.

3.19   MRPII is often described as a closed-loop system, in that there is an automatic feedback from the manufacturing function to the MPS, leading to changes in the MPS. This in turn leads to adjustments in manufacturing plans, thus closing the information loop as illustrated in Figure 3.5.

Figure 3.5 *A closed-loop MRP II system*

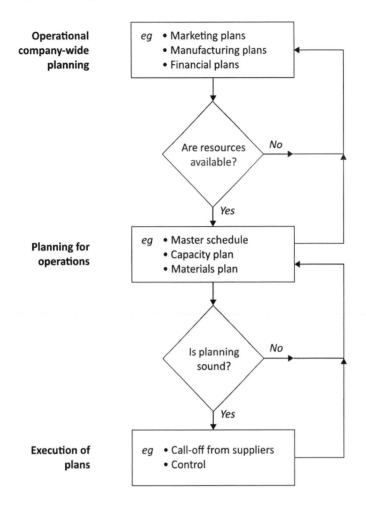

3.20 Closing the loop involves comparing production plans against the availability of resources. MRP makes the assumption that resources required are available. Closed loop MRPII checks whether the required resources are available. If this is not the case then the MPS is modified.

3.21 MRP and MRPII systems have proven themselves particularly in batch manufacture. Although they require ongoing investment in people and system development the rewards in increased professionalism as the system integrates into the organisation can be impressive.

3.22 Manufacturing on a larger scale brings a new range of issues that goes beyond the design of MRP and MRPII systems. Just in time (JIT) systems can utilise MRP and MRPII, but MRP shows to best advantage in batch production systems where the need is to schedule production around customer demand and supplier lead times.

4   Just in time supply and *kanban* systems

Eliminating waste

4.1   The concept of just in time (JIT) is concerned with the reduction and ultimately the elimination of waste. It is often linked to the concept of **lean supply** – 'lean' meaning more efficient and less wasteful.

Kanban systems

4.2   This simply means 'communication' and is the physical means of transmitting requirements to suppliers. It can be achieved electronically, by telephone or fax, or by any other means deemed suitable by both parties. Alternatively, it can simply tell the warehouse manager or personnel that an item needs re-ordering. It could do this by giving an electronic signal when a despatch is made that takes the item's stock to below where it should be. Upon receipt of the signal an order for replenishment of the stock item would be placed with the supplier.

4.3   The **two-bin system** is a much older, more traditional version of *kanban*. The two-bin approach is probably the simplest form of stock control and stock replenishment, and it operates purely visually. Each item is physically stored in two bins. When the first bin is empty this is a signal that replenishment is required and an order is placed with the supplier. While the order is arriving, the second bin is used. The only possible pitfall with this system is that storekeepers need to be trained only to take items from the first bin until it is empty – if they take items from both bins at the same time, problems could result.

4.4   There are two variations on the theme.

- Both bins are of the same size and hold the same amount of items. When the first bin is empty, re-ordering takes place. When the second bin is empty, this again triggers the ordering process and items from the first bin are used until it in turn is empty. In other words, this is a kind of 'revolving' process.
- The second bin is tailored to hold the amount of stock required in order to see the company through the supplier's lead-time period so that the goods should arrive at about the same time as the second bin becomes empty. In this variation, which could be seen as a slightly more refined version, the first bin is the 'main' one with the second being seen as buffer stock. The order quantity must be sufficient to replenish both bins.

4.5   Waste (especially in terms of excess production) is hugely expensive. The more accurate the demand forecast, the greater the profitability. If demand is not forecast accurately then the result is customer dissatisfaction. Manufacturing companies that are working towards JIT increasingly require deliveries to be made from suppliers direct to the production area.

4.6   This demand-led manufacturing is known as a **pull system**: goods are pulled into stock only when they are needed. The manufacturer aims to produce goods only against known customer orders. With this system there is greater certainty; deliveries, storage and movement to the production line can be accurately planned. JIT is also common in the retail sector, particularly in large supermarket operations. Overall, JIT can be described as a system whereby stocks are pulled through the supply chain by customers.

4.7   In a pull system, storage is integrated by using the *kanban* system. This can be described as 'ordering a box, when one is left on the line'. This two-bin approach replaces the used item with another when the first item has been used. With more general items a minimum quantity (eg 30 items) is held in a tote box. When the 30 units have been used the second box comes forward. The original box is then replenished.

Responsive suppliers

4.8 The JIT concept is a move towards reducing supplier lead times, buyer stockholdings and work in progress. It is based on a positive inventory management policy and needs close cooperation from suppliers to be successful. Whilst the ultimate objective is zero stockholding for the buyer, it is clear that optimum performance could be difficult to achieve unless the supplier holds stocks of the required components. However, reduced delivery times of acceptable specified quality items, as in the MRP system, would result in reduced stockholdings and investment.

4.9 Making this concept work satisfactorily requires reliable and responsive suppliers. This means that, when selecting a supplier, thorough evaluation is essential. This may lead if necessary to **supplier development**: a positive policy of the buying company in extending practical support and assistance to the supplier. It is often said that JIT can be achieved by developing a very close and ongoing relationship with suppliers, supported by the linking of relevant IT systems enabling suppliers to see the customers' production schedules and rate of manufacture and to tailor their production accordingly.

4.10 The facility provided by the supplier in holding stock for JIT delivery would no doubt result in an increased component price, but this would be offset by the reduction of stockholding costs at the buyer's company and the assurance of on-time delivery.

4.11 In JIT systems the demand information comes directly from the purchasing organisation to the supplying organisation. JIT is not a programme for suppliers only, but will only effectively work if the buyer and supplier work as a partnership. Because it requires absolute minimum stocks and reliance, normally, on a sole supplier per type of goods, the information relative to, say, daily requirements has to be notified as accurately and as soon as possible to the supplier. This may mean that the situation is relayed electronically, and an EDI system may be the ideal medium.

4.12 In order to meet frequent orders, the supplier needs the purchaser to forecast demands in advance and notify actual demands as soon as is practical, especially if they deviate significantly from those forecast. Demand information then has to be given within the supplier organisation, to ensure the right quantity of materials is available and is despatched to arrive according to the scheduled requirements. Consignment stocking or VMI (see later in this chapter) could also be useful here.

4.13 The purchasing organisation also has to ensure that it is able to manage and identify what it actually does require and when it requires it. This demands that the organisation has a system for identifying material usage, which is its commitment to the suppliers. The system works because the demand for producing a unit pulls work through. This can be an operation-by-operation pull in the purchasing organisation. If there is no pull, then there is no requirement for the goods.

4.14 JIT requires that the organisation realises what to produce, and the time taken in each phase of production. JIT systems provide the best current application of stock control systems but rely heavily on management commitment and technology to make the operation work. Stock is delivered 'just in time' for manufacture.

4.15 Clearly a JIT system means that there is little margin for error. The product quality must be high and 'fit for purpose' as there is no margin for goods being rejected or reworked. This is a concept known as 'zero defects'. Delivery must be on time, every time and in consequence, many suppliers are situated geographically close to their customers.

4.16 In order to be able to achieve JIT much emphasis is placed on having suppliers of the highest possible standard in all aspects of their performance. For this reason, it might be useful for manufacturing companies that are employing JIT to involve suppliers of components and materials at the design and development stage of their product. This might involve sharing commercially sensitive information. This is another reason why supplier evaluation and the development of close supplier relationships would be important.

4.17 In the retail sector, organisations using JIT would need to share sales forecast information and usage figures to enable suppliers to schedule deliveries efficiently.

JIT and MRP

4.18 JIT and MRP can be used together. The MPS forecasts projected total demand for the manufacturing company's product but individual components are 'pulled' through the system, on a JIT basis, as they are required.

4.19 A variation on the JIT theme is **late customisation**. This refers to a manufacturing process where the final processes ('finishing touches') of a product's manufacture are delayed until the customer's exact requirements are known. The example invariably quoted in the literature is that of Dell Computers. A customer ordering a Dell computer provides details of his requirements online. Most of the components required for a computer have already been produced and assembled. Dell then completes the manufacture of the computer in line with the specific order requirements and despatches it to the customer.

4.20 To make such a system work, the manufacturer (Dell is only an example – there are others) must have JIT supplies from its suppliers. If not, it would not be able to produce in line with customer requirements and despatch its finished product to customers, all with very little notice. In such situations, it is the JIT concept and the use of efficient, reliable, suppliers that enable it to work.

JIT and ABC analysis

4.21 We can also make a connection between just in time and ABC (stock category) analysis, because:

- Investment in JIT would not be worthwhile for all categories of stock: using ABC analysis, JIT effort can be prioritised and focused on suitable stock categories.
- ABC analysis can be applied to both value and volume issues to increase the efficiency and effectiveness of stores making possible further improvements via JIT, which would be difficult to achieve with a chaotic stores system.

4.22 For Category A high-value items and/or bulky items that take up significant storage space, for example, an organisation would benefit greatly from operating a pull system such as JIT, and only bringing the stock into the organisation when it was required. This would optimise space utilisation and minimise the opportunity cost of having capital tied up in high-value stock.

Advantages and disadvantages of JIT

4.23 The advantages and disadvantages of JIT are summarised in Table 3.2. We should note that in general, the disadvantages are considered to be outweighed by the potential advantages and cost savings.

Table 3.2 *Advantages and disadvantages of JIT*

ADVANTAGES	DISADVANTAGES
Reducing wastes, maximising added value and minimising costs	Vulnerability to supplier or system failure: no time or stock buffers
Flexibility to meet variable demands and contingencies, through the development of swift response	Potential reduction in production capacity utilisation (traded off with flexibility, customer satisfaction)
Reduced stock levels and lead times, higher quality (required to maintain speed of delivery to customer) and therefore better customer service	Higher price charged by suppliers for delivering on a JIT basis, plus possibly loss of bulk discounts (due to smaller orders).
Employee involvement and empowerment, potentially leading to commitment and proactive improvements	Smaller, more frequent orders (if not organised on the basis of 'call-off' contracts), resulting in higher order costs.
Improved supply chain relationships, and integrated systems	Additional costs of monitoring and managing supplier performance, reliability and quality

4.24 JIT is not appropriate for every organisation, or in all circumstances. There may be problems for a company seeking to operate JIT direct with an overseas supplier, for example, due to:

- Difficulty of developing close collaboration and trust with suppliers, given limited opportunities for communication and interaction
- Difficulties and costs of monitoring supplier performance and quality, given the distance to the supply market (particularly in countries where quality standards are generally lower or less regulated)
- Long delivery lead times, due to the distance goods have to be transported
- Loss of efficiency of transport capacity utilisation, delivering more frequent, smaller consignments
- Increased risk of supply disruption, due to transport risk, environmental risks in the foreign supply market and so on.

4.25 Potential disadvantages of JIT can be summarised as follows.

- It might be necessary to pay a higher unit price for items to suppliers to compensate for the supplier's costs in supplying on a JIT basis. This should be outweighed, however, by the greatly reduced cost of storage that should arise from the use of JIT.
- Following from that, the buyer might lose bulk discounts from suppliers because of small quantities being delivered at any one time. This should not be the case, however, if the buyer is able to forecast total requirements with reasonable accuracy.
- There is great reliance placed on suppliers who must be able to deliver in the ways mentioned above (in terms of quality, time, etc). This is not a disadvantage in itself although, if suppliers let the buyer down, there would be significant problems of lost or delayed production. This is probably the biggest potential disadvantage of JIT.
- Further to this last issue, there might be a cost associated with the evaluation and monitoring of suppliers to ensure their reliability. Again, however, this should be more than outweighed by the advantages that arise from JIT.

5   Consignment stocking and VMI

Introduction

5.1   Stock control and replenishment combines important elements of the management and control of stocks. The aim is to ensure that we do not carry too much stock but equally that we do not run out of stock. Stock control systems achieve this by indicating when we need to re-order materials.

5.2   Within any stock control system consideration must be given to the cost of stockouts. These situations can occur if the re-ordering systems have not been fully considered and implemented. In this section of the chapter we look at various ways in which stock levels can be controlled.

Consignment stocking systems

5.3   Consignment stocking is a method of purchase that can help a buyer with cashflow problems. It involves making an agreement with a supplier that they will supply an initial quantity of an item. They will then monitor usage of the item and 'top up' stocks in line with the buyer's usage. This means that the buyer will not run out of stock of the item. It also has the advantage that payment is only made when the item is issued from stock, not when it is received into the buyer's warehouse.

5.4   This is a 'streamlining' system whereby the supplier deposits goods directly into the buyer's stores. The buying company only pays for the goods they have actually used. This helps reduce the cost of storage significantly by, in effect, eliminating the opportunity cost of storage.

5.5   The supplier visits the customer on a periodic basis to check stock levels. Alternatively, the supplier might be given access to the purchasing company's electronic stock records of the items concerned. This might be done via an extranet system.

5.6   Stock is then replenished to the agreed level and the company is invoiced for the goods used. The goods in stock remain the property of the supplier until they are used. A single contract covers the whole process. This indicates price, code of item and description. The buyers exercise control by auditing the level of usage periodically to minimise the risk of a stockout.

Vendor managed inventory

5.7   This works in a very similar manner to consignment stocking except that the supplier keeps the stock at their premises awaiting call-off by the buyer. Suppliers will usually request a forecast of usage before agreeing to set up a system such as this. The forecast might take the form of a projection of total annual usage although much depends on whether or not the item can easily be sold to other customers. From the buyer's viewpoint it is important that a supplier offering this service guarantees that, once called off, supplies will be at the buyer's premises within a short space of time (eg 48 hours).

5.8   The benefits of vendor managed inventory (VMI) can be summarised as follows.

- The vendor is given access to information (production plans, inventory, ordering, sales forecasts), which may enable it to improve service levels in various ways. It may also benefit from the ability to optimise its internal capacity utilisation and materials flow.
- Responsibility is delegated to the vendor to store, manage and replenish the buyer's

inventory, within policy guidelines: this should result in administrative savings for the buyer, without incurring major risk. This makes VMI a low-maintenance approach to managing low-priority stocks (eg Category C).

- Buyers benefit from the freedom to focus on more strategic decision-making
- Buyers usually require a guarantee of short-lead-time delivery following call-off orders, creating a strong performance incentive for suppliers.

Chapter summary

- Pareto analysis is based on the principle that a small number of stock items may account for a large proportion of total stock value.
- ABC analysis extends this idea to classify stocks in order of their usage value. Managerial attention is devoted mainly to the stock items with high usage value.
- Some stock items are subject to independent demand: usage does not depend on demand for anything else. Items are subject to dependent demand if usage depends on the quantity demanded of something else.
- To control inventory of dependent demand items we use techniques such as MRP and MRPII. Both are based on producing a master production schedule which is then 'exploded' to produce a bill of materials.
- Just in time purchasing and supply is concerned with reducing and eventually eliminating waste in the supply chain.
- *Kanban* systems are a method of achieving just in time supply. Their success depends on finding responsive suppliers who can supply the right quality of materials promptly.
- Consignment stocking enables a buying organisation to improve cashflow. The buyer does not pay for supplies until they are actually used.
- Vendor managed inventory goes one step further than consignment stocking. The buyer does not even take delivery of the stock until it is needed. Until then, it remains on the supplier's premises.

 ## Self-test questions

Numbers in brackets refer to the paragraphs above where your answers can be checked.

1   Explain the Pareto principle. (1.4, 1.5)

2   Explain the use of ABC analysis in stock control. (1.6)

3   What is meant by stock turnover? (1.11)

4   Distinguish between dependent and independent demand. (2.2, 2.3)

5   How is a master production schedule produced? (3.2)

6   How is a bill of materials produced from a master production schedule? (3.5)

7   List advantages of MRP. (3.11)

8   Distinguish between MRP and MRPII. (3.14)

9   Explain how a two-bin system works. (4.3)

10   What is meant by supplier development? (4.9)

11   List advantages and disadvantages of just in time purchasing. (Table 3.2)

12   Distinguish between consignment stocking and VMI. (5.7)

CHAPTER 4

Calculating Demand for Inventory

Assessment criteria and indicative content

 1.4 Analyse the main techniques for calculating the future demand of inventory

- Economic order quantity
- Reorder point and periodic review systems
- MRP and MRPII
- The bullwhip effect
- Qualitative and quantitative approaches to forecasting

Section headings

1. Demand, usage and lead times
2. Stock replenishment systems
3. The economic order quantity
4. Approaches to forecasting

1 Demand, usage and lead times

Stock control

1.1 In this chapter we will consider one of the most important aspects of securing supply: that of stock control and stock replenishment. Stock control and replenishment essentially involve ensuring that we have enough stock (without overstocking) and triggering the ordering process for new deliveries when we realise that we are running out of stock.

1.2 This might suggest a fairly haphazard approach but nothing could be further from the truth. This is particularly true in large warehouses where a wide range of items might be stocked. As we have seen in previous chapters, the cost of storage is potentially high and therefore we need to minimise stockholding as much as possible. However, as we have also seen, the cost of not having adequate stocks can be even higher. This means that we must monitor demand and usage of items closely and then be able to re-order supplies when necessary.

1.3 Stock control has been defined as 'the systematic regulation of stock levels with respect to time and quantity.'

1.4 We can therefore summarise the main purposes of a stock control system as follows.

- To indicate **when** an item should be made or bought by monitoring the movement of materials and goods in and out of stores
- To assist in deciding the **quantity** to be bought or made
- To regulate the level of stock for each item so that stockouts and excess stocks are avoided, but costs incurred by the company in investment in stocks are minimised

- To minimise stockholding while still meeting customer service needs. This is a difficult balance to achieve as low stocks, while saving on capital outlay and associated storage costs, may not enable customer service levels to be met. On the other hand, high stocks may mean the ability to offer high levels of customer service but potentially at a high cost
- To maintain perpetual stock records which enable stock levels to be regulated and/or checked at any time

1.5 We have two terms that are very similar but require some explanation.

- **Demand**: this refers to the requirements of customers and is typically, but not exclusively, used to refer to external customers. Usually we are interested in predicting future demand, which will involve forecasting techniques (see later in this chapter).
- **Usage**: this refers to actual usage of items that is happening now, from day to day. It usually refers to internal customers and details of it can often be obtained from the organisation's records of activities.

1.6 Not all stock is the same in its nature and purpose. Some items may be held as a buffer or as insurance against market shortages, while other items may be routine purchases available at short-notice delivery from suppliers. Some items tie up more capital than others. Some are required to meet seasonal fluctuations. Management of the stock range involves balancing these factors to ensure that customer service requirements can be met at an affordable cost.

1.7 If demand and/or usage of items is steady and predictable, stock control is relatively straightforward. If 100 units of an item are demanded and used each week, we need to ensure that we have 100 units of that item at the beginning of each week. Assuming there is no problem with the supplier's lead time, this would not be difficult.

1.8 Unfortunately, things are seldom as straightforward as we would like. Demand and/or the rate of usage might vary. If variations are predictable, we can ensure that stock levels rise and fall in line with demand. The problems occur when demand and/or usage are unpredictable. In such situations, it would be necessary to hold buffer stocks (sometimes known as 'safety stocks').

1.9 Buffer stocks are stocks held just in case demand or usage suddenly and unpredictably increases. The more unpredictable the demand or usage, the greater the need to hold buffer stocks and the greater the quantity of buffer stocks needed.

1.10 However, much depends here upon lead time. The implications of this are much the same as for demand and usage. If lead time is predictable and short, then items can be purchased quickly to cope with a sudden increase in demand. If lead time is long and/or unpredictable, this course of action would not be possible and large buffer stocks would need to be held in case of demand surges.

1.11 What should be apparent from this is that lead time issues must be considered against demand issues and the whole question must be considered 'in the round'. Where both demand and lead time are unpredictable, buffer stocks will need to be high. Failing that, the likelihood of stocking out, with its consequences (halting of operations and supply to customers etc), will be serious.

1.12 In this situation, the cost of storage will be high but as we have already seen, is likely to be outweighed by the cost of having to halt operations. We illustrate such situations in Figure 4.1.

Figure 4.1 *Factors affecting the need to hold stock*

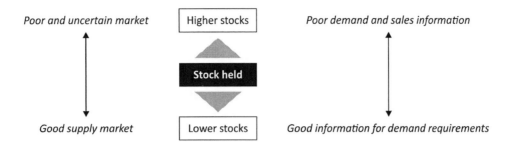

1.13 The factors illustrated in Figure 4.1 are further elaborated in Table 4.1.

Table 4.1 *Conditions affecting the need to hold stock*

CONDITION	CONTRIBUTING FACTORS
Poor and uncertain supply market	• Seasonality • Scarcity • Insensitive monopoly supplier
Poor demand, planning and sales information	• Lack of co-ordination between departments • Marketing not understanding the needs of production • Lack of systems
Good supply market	• Can help reduce stocks • Helps develop supplier partnerships on supply and demand • Helps get nearer to JIT stock
Good information for demand requirements	• Gives confidence to lower stockholding buffer on risk material • Aids the corporate planning process through the whole organisation • Good production scheduling systems even out demand in a planned way

1.14 In summary, what we have to do is to analyse both demand and lead-time characteristics of each of the items we keep in stock and try to ensure that we have adequate stocks to cover all eventualities. This might be easier said than done but we will consider techniques that can assist this process later in this chapter.

2 Stock replenishment systems

2.1 The aim of stock management, for independent demand items, is to set up a regular system for monitoring levels of stock, and planning to replenish them in time to meet forecast demand (the right quantity at the right time) – while generally carrying as little stock as possible. There are two main methods for doing this.

- Periodic review systems, in which the stock level of an item is reviewed at regular or fixed intervals, and, depending on the quantity in stock, a replenishment order is placed for whatever quantity appears to be appropriate.
- Fixed order point systems, in which stock of an item is replenished with a predetermined quantity when inventory falls to a predetermined re-order level (ROL) or fixed order point

2.2 Let's look at each of these approaches in turn.

Periodic review

2.3 In periodic review systems (also called fixed interval ordering, scheduling systems or 'topping up' systems), the stock level of the product is examined on a periodic (fixed time interval) basis, and, depending on the quantity in stock, a replenishment order is placed to 'top up' stock to the desired level. In other words, the order quantity is not fixed, but the timing of orders is. Replenishment quantities vary, being whatever is sufficient to bring stock levels up to a predetermined stock level – or whatever is needed to last through the next interval, or until the next delivery. This can be depicted simply as follows: Figure 4.2.

Figure 4.2 *Periodic review system*

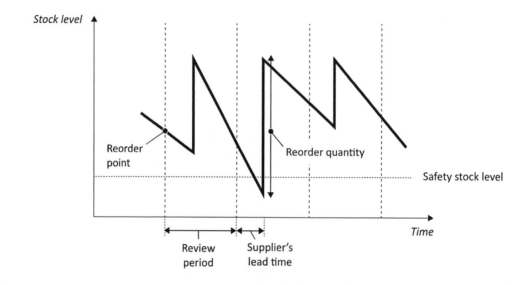

2.4 The length of the review period will be determined on an item-by-item (or category-by-category) basis, depending on usage patterns. The shorter the review period, the more effort and cost is involved, so it is usual to apply an ABC analysis: Category A items might be reviewed weekly, Category B items monthly and Category C items quarterly, say.

2.5 The review itself can be undertaken by periodic physical inspection by stores staff ('stocktake'), or by a computerised or manual system that records ongoing purchases, requisitions and returns of each item to give a running total of stock held at any given time. (This latter system is sometimes called **perpetual inventory**, because it is carried out on a constant basis.)

2.6 Computerised systems often use barcode scanning to input stock data to the system. A more modern alternative is **radio frequency identification** (RFID): an electronic tagging system which does not require item-by-item scanning to input stock data, but simply 'reads' the signals given out by electronic tags on stock.

2.7 Once the current stock level has been established at a given review point, the decision must be taken on how much to order to replenish the stock to a desired level. Take a monthly review system, for example. At the 1st January review point, an order will be made based on the quantities of the item likely to be required during January; *plus* enough stock to cover the lead time for delivery following a review and order on the 1st February; *plus* an appropriate level of safety stock.

2.8 In other words, the size of the order will be calculated as: forecast demand over the forthcoming review interval; *plus* forecast demand over the lead time for replenishment (ordering and delivery) in the following review interval; *plus* safety or buffer stock; minus current stock levels; minus stock already on order but not yet delivered.

2.9 The *advantages* and *disadvantages* of a periodic review or fixed interval ordering system are shown in Table 4.2.

Table 4.2 *Advantages and disadvantages of periodic review systems*

ADVANTAGES	DISADVANTAGES
Ease of administration and control, with predictable workload planning for purchasing and warehousing staff (at fixed review and replenishment periods)	The risk of unexpected stockouts, since the system assumes that there will be no review of stock other than at the fixed interval. This necessitates the use of safety stocks.
Orders may be placed at the same time for a number of items, enabling the consolidation of shipments, reduced transport costs, or quantity discounts from suppliers	Higher average stocks than with fixed order point systems, because of the need to provide for review periods, lead times and safety stocks
Ability to identify slow-moving or obsolete stock items, due to periodic stock review.	Re-order quantities not based on economic order quantities (EOQs – see later in this chapter)
	Waste of time reviewing stock levels which do not require action.

Fixed order point and re-order level (ROL)

2.10 In a fixed order point (or re-order point) system, stock of an item is replenished with a predetermined (fixed order) quantity when inventory falls to a predetermined minimum level (the re-order level or ROL). In other words – directly opposite to the periodic review approach – the timing of the order isn't fixed, but the quantity is. The system can be depicted simply as follows: Figure 4.3.

Figure 4.3 *Fixed order point systems*

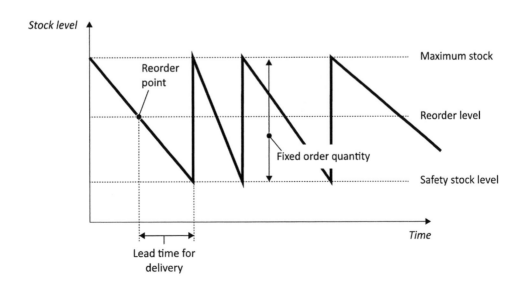

2.11 To determine the re-order point for a particular item, managers rely on past experience of demand and usage patterns for the item, taking into account any known factors which may lessen or increase demand or usage in the coming period. The aim is to fix on a stock level sufficient to keep the business in stock during the supplier's delivery lead time, plus a reserve of safety stock. In other words, a basic re-order level (ROL) should be equal to:

- Maximum amount used × maximum lead time for replenishment; *or*
- Average amount used × average lead time + safety stock

2.12 Once stock falls to this predetermined order point or ROL, the system triggers a replenishment order.

- A common manual method for doing this is a two-bin system. We described this in the previous chapter.
- Computerised perpetual inventory systems (using barcoding or RFID to record inputs and withdrawals of stock and maintain running totals) may be used to automatically trigger replenishment orders when inventory has fallen to the specified re-order point.

2.13 In either case, the re-order quantity is the same each time. For items of high value, it may be sensible to use a structured approach to determining what this quantity should be, perhaps by using the economic order quantity (EOQ) – described below. For small-value items, simple decision rules (based on usage rates) may be more cost-effective.

2.14 Advantages and disadvantages of a fixed order quantity or ROL system are summarised in Table 4.3.

Table 4.3 *Advantages and disadvantages of fixed order point systems*

ADVANTAGES	DISADVANTAGES
Ability to use the EOQ, unlike periodic review systems	Acceptance of the holding cost (which may be expensive if the stock levels are set too high)
Lower average levels of stock than with periodic review systems, because of enhanced responsiveness to demand fluctuations	Assumption that stock usage patterns and lead times are predictable and stable. Parameters must be reviewed, to avoid risk of stockouts (if demand is higher, or lead time longer, than foreseen) – or excess stock (eg if replenished in full, despite fall-off of demand).
Automatic 'triggering' of replenishment by the system, without time being wasted on items where the stock level is satisfactory.	Inefficiencies, from inappropriate order points and quantities and/or from ordering of individual items at different times. Eg: frequent uneconomical small orders.
	Risk of overloading purchasing systems and staff, if multiple items reach their re-order levels at the same time.

3 The economic order quantity

3.1 We mentioned in a previous chapter that there is a trade-off between holding costs and acquisition costs of stock. As buyers, we wish to minimise the total of these costs by ordering the optimum level of stock, known as the economic order quantity or EOQ. This is illustrated in Figure 4.4.

Figure 4.4 *The economic order quantity (EOQ) model*

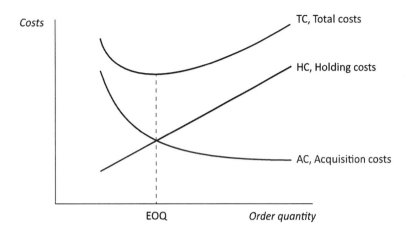

- The HC line slopes steadily upwards from left to right, because the higher the order quantity, the higher the stock levels – and the higher the holding costs.
- The AC line slopes down from left to right, because the higher the order quantity, the fewer orders will be placed, and the lower the acquisition costs.
- The TC line is derived simply by totalling the holding costs and acquisition costs at each point along the horizontal (order quantity) axis. The lowest point on this line represents the point of lowest total cost – and this corresponds to the order quantity at which HC and AC intersect: ie where acquisition costs equal holding costs. (This can be proved mathematically, but you do not need to know the detail.)

3.2 There are various ways of calculating EOQ mathematically. The simplest formula is:

$$EOQ = \sqrt{\frac{2cd}{h}}$$

where 'c' represents the cost of making an order, 'd' represents the estimated demand for (usage of) the item in the relevant period, and 'h' represents the cost of holding one unit of the item in stock for the relevant period.

3.3 Say the cost of making an order for widgets is $50; the annual usage rate is 1,500 widgets per year; and the cost of holding one widget in stock for a year is $2.

$$EOQ = \sqrt{\frac{2 \times \$50 \times 1,500}{2}} = \sqrt{75,000} = 274$$

In practice, this would probably mean an EOQ of 300 widgets, which would be ordered five times per year (to make up the requirement of 1,500 widgets in total).

3.4 You might notice that the EOQ formula makes no reference at all to the largest component of stock costs: the actual purchase price of the stock item! The reason for this is that purchase prices are assumed to be constant, regardless of the order quantity, and therefore are not relevant to the decision. Clearly, this is a simplifying assumption. (In practice, there may be supplier discounts for larger order quantities, for example.)

3.5 The EOQ model is helpful in establishing the most economical order quantity for high-value items, as part of a fixed order quantity system. However, it does suffer from certain limitations.

- It is based on assumptions about the consistency of demand, order quantities and supplier lead times – which may not always be valid in practice.
- It is a cumbersome method to apply, and should only be used if justified by the value of the item being examined.
- Some of the costs (such as clerical time, interest rates and order costs) are difficult to estimate.
- The model does not take into account price breaks and bulk discounts – nor other factors in optimum order quantities, such as the perishability of stocks, or the transport efficiencies of larger orders.
- There are usually fixed elements in order or storage costs, so that these will not vary directly with the number of orders placed or the volume of stock held.
- Storage space may be strictly limited, so it may not be possible to order the amount indicated by the EOQ formula.
- The formula does not take account of shelf-life of items in stock
- The formula does not take account of transport requirements. For example, it might result in a quantity that only fills a small part of a lorry but you might have to pay the supplier for a load that fills the whole lorry.
- It involves an element of stocks being held 'just in case' which goes against the move in some organisations towards 'just in time' and lean supply.

3.6   The EOQ estimation can be modified to take account of some of these limitations. The point to emphasise again is that the re-order quantity should not be decided without careful reference to all the costs involved.

4   Approaches to forecasting

Introduction

4.1   In order to manage stocks and ensure that we turn stock over efficiently, we need to consider demand, usage and lead time. Where these are fixed, as they sometimes are, there is no problem. However, as we have seen, they are often unpredictable. In such situations, we need to be able to **forecast** our requirements as well as the lead time of items required in order to plan stock levels and stock turnover. In this section we will consider how forecasting might be carried out.

4.2   Customer service can be addressed by forecasting what products customers will want and manufacturing or holding stock to meet the forecast. The key to having the right inventory in the warehouse is to forecast and make, or buy in, the right product. The accuracy of the demand forecast is vital but is difficult to ensure. Forecasts are effective in certain areas such as predicting stable demand, tracking sales trends, dealing with seasonality and projecting the effects of cyclical changes. They are not so effective when demand and/or supply is erratic.

4.3   Forecasting is a key element in effective inventory management. The main element in forecasting is 'prediction'; to make effective predictions of future requirements is key to the whole process.

4.4   Predictions are generally made by using the following sources of information.

- Historical usage data
- Current data and information such as that available from suppliers on usage
- What is happening within the marketplace
- Any future predictions based on supply and demand.

4.5 For example if product prices are falling demand may increase, whereas if product prices are rising demand may fall. Rising demand may lead to stockouts and supply shortage problems, whereas falling demand may lead to slow moving and obsolete stocks. Therefore all forecasts and predictions require constant revision in order to maximise their accuracy.

4.6 Forecasting is the process of estimating future quantities required, using past experience as a basis. It is fairly easy to predict the pattern of demand for some stock lines. For example, if an item is obsolete, demand will almost certainly decline as time progresses. If a special sales campaign is to be started, demand should rise. Seasonal items, such as Christmas decorations or fans for the summer, will have a fluctuating demand. Very often, however, the position is not so obvious, and can only be found by keeping records of past performance and projecting them into the future by forecasting. We now describe some methods of doing this.

Simple moving average (or moving straight average)

4.7 As the name suggests, this is a simple technique. All we do is to look at the demand for recent periods, and assume that demand for the coming period will be the average of that experienced in the past. There is no particular rule about how many past periods we should take into account. If we are trying to estimate demand during July we might, for example, look at the actual demand experienced during January to June, and take the average of those six months.

4.8 Suppose that usage of an independent demand material was as follows in the months of January to June.

Month	Usage in litres
January	450
February	190
March	600
April	600
May	420
June	380
Total usage January to June	2,640

4.9 Using a simple moving average we would simply take the average of these six months: 2,640/6 = 440 litres. This would be our estimate of usage in July.

4.10 The reason for the term 'moving' average is that each month we move along by one step. Thus in estimating usage for August, we discard the January figure above and replace it with the figure for actual usage in July. Our estimate for August is therefore based on the six months preceding August, namely February to July.

4.11 Of course, this procedure is really a bit too simple. It is clear from the figures that demand for this material fluctuates quite markedly. The figures for January to June show a low of 190 litres, and a high of 600 litres. The simple average of such figures does not inspire confidence. The actual figure in July might turn out to be either of these extremes, in which case our estimate of 440 litres will prove wide of the mark. The next method tries to inject greater sophistication into the estimates.

Weighted average method (or moving weighted average)

4.12 The simple moving average gives equal weight to each of the figures recorded in previous periods. In the example, the figure for January contributed exactly as much to the averaging calculation as did that for June. This does not take account of a fact which is very commonly observed in practice, namely that older figures are a less reliable guide to the future than more recent figures. If there is any gradual change taking place in our pattern of usage of the item, it is more likely that the change will be reflected in our usage for June than in the figure for January six months ago.

4.13 To take account of this, the technique of moving weighted average can be used. This is designed to give greater weight to the figures experienced in recent months, and to reduce the weight given to older figures.

4.14 In our earlier example, suppose that we decide to base our estimate for July on just the four previous months (March to June inclusive). We could recognise the higher importance of recent months by giving a weighting of 0.4 to the June figure, 0.3 to May, 0.2 to April and 0.1 to March. (These weightings are not fixed – we can exercise judgement in fixing them – but they must always total to 1 if the arithmetic is to make sense.)

4.15 Our estimate for July would then be calculated as follows:

$(0.4 \times 380) + (0.3 \times 420) + (0.2 \times 600) + (0.1 \times 600) = 458$ litres

Trend analysis

4.16 **Trend analysis** is another way of making forecasting predictions. Here, the information used to make forecasts is 'subjective' rather than the 'objective' data above. There are four basic patterns of demand.

- **Steady trend**: An increase or decline in demand is moving with a predictable pace that can easily be forecast.
- **Fluctuating trend**: The rise or fall in demand is volatile or unstable and reliable predictions are therefore difficult to achieve.
- **Rising trend**: Demand rises at a steady pace and can easily be forecast on historical data; this may have implications for material supply if demand continues to rise.
- **Falling trend**: Demand falls at a steady pace and can easily be forecast on historical data; this may have implications for stocks becoming slow moving or obsolete.

4.17 However sophisticated the system of forecasting may be, it will not be 100 per cent accurate and there will be a difference between forecast and actual usage. This is known as **forecast error** or **forecast deviation**, and allowance must be made for it. In a perfect situation where the forecast was 100 per cent correct every time, and where the supplier always delivered promptly, the pattern of stock would be in perfect flowing lines of supply and demand.

4.18 Safety stock is related to the accuracy of forecasting, and in fact depends on the forecast error. If the forecast error is large, the safety stock will also have to be large and if the error is small, a low safety stock is indicated. The level of service desired must also be taken into account. At a service level of 98%, there should be 98 chances in 100 that stock will be available when called for. It might be impracticable to aim for100% service, but the higher the service level the more safety stock will be needed.

4.19 Stock control systems based on the weighted average method of forecasting are most satisfactory when applied to finished goods held for distribution or for resale. Simple forecasting techniques are not usually suitable for the control of raw materials and bought-out parts for manufacturing organisations or construction companies, where demand is strictly related to a pre-planned operational programme. Even in these firms, however, it may usefully be applied to general consumable stores.

4.20 In situations where demand is independent (ie demand for one items bears no relationship to the demand for other items), decisions as to how much to stock will be based on the inventory manager's view of the probabilities of different levels of demand arising. These probabilities will, to some extent, be subjective, ie some measure of opinion or judgment will be employed in their determination.

4.21 Accuracy of forecasts is, of course, variable. A manufacturer's annual production plan would be expected to be more accurate than a hotel's forecast of annual guest numbers, for example. Forecasting is particularly important in the retail sector where a forecast, not only of annual sales of an item but also seasonal variations would be required. Many companies use sophisticated computer packages to carry out this kind of forecasting. Inventory, of course, is purchased based on the forecast and held until it is required.

The Delphi method

4.22 So far we have been discussing **quantitative** (numerical) techniques for forecasting demand. More subjective (**qualitative**) methods can also be used. For example, we can attempt to predict demand by gathering expert opinion (from buyers, suppliers and other knowledgeable people). The value of the contributors and the judgement made can be called into question, but knowledge and experience will usually provide a sound basis on which to develop a forecast.

4.23 The method of using experts is frequently criticised. The 'Delphi' method (originally developed in 1944), in essence seeks to impose a statistical rigour and to counter the argument of bias that frequently accompanies the gathering and use of 'expert opinion'.

4.24 The term Delphi refers to the site of the most revered oracle in ancient Greece. The objective of the Delphi method is the reliable and creative development of ideas or the production of suitable information to aid decision-making.

4.25 The Delphi method involves group communication by experts who are geographically dispersed. Questionnaires are sent to the selected experts by post or email and are designed to elicit and develop individual responses to the problems posed. The responses are considered and refined with subsequent questionnaires to develop a group response.

4.26 A main consideration of the Delphi method is to overcome the disadvantages of conventional committee action where individuals may dominate, bias may develop or groups may polarise in their thinking. The group interaction in Delphi is anonymous, as comments made are not identified to their originator. A panel director or monitor, whose role is to focus the group on the stated objectives, controls the interaction between group members.

4.27 To operate successfully the participants should understand the process and aim of the exercise although there is some debate on the level of expertise required from the 'sages'. Armstrong and Welty suggest that a high degree of expertise is not necessary while Hanson and Ramani state that the respondents should be well informed in the appropriate area.

4.28 The Delphi method has proved useful in answering specific, single-dimension questions. There is less support for its use to determine more complex forecasts that involve multiple factors.

The bullwhip effect

4.29 The bullwhip effect (also known as the **Forrester effect**) is an important concept that highlights the importance of sharing forecast sales and production information with suppliers and other trading partners along the supply chain. It has been observed that, in traditional supply chains, a small change in final consumer demand leads to a much bigger change in demand 'upstream' in the supply chain. We may explain the Forrester effect by means of a simple example.

4.30 Airline ABC orders 10 aircraft from aircraft manufacturer XYZ for delivery in 12 months. Aircraft manufacturer XYZ is not expecting the order and is, of course, delighted to oblige an important customer. To ensure they do not let the customer down, and just in case they want a little extra, XYZ orders 24 wings from the wing supplier, and not the actual 20 required.

4.31 The wing supplier needs to buy two fuel tanks for each wing to be manufactured. Thinking in the same way as the aircraft manufacturer, he orders 60 fuel tanks from the fuel tank supplier and not 48 (and certainly not the actual 40 required). Assuming that the fuel tank manufacturer needs two fuel pumps for each tank the fuel pump supplier behaves in the same way as the others and orders 160 pumps rather than 120, and so on up the chain....

4.32 Thus, we have the fuel pump manufacturer gearing up to manufacture 160 pumps when in fact only 80 will be actually used. This is the Forrester effect.

4.33 The fuel pump manufacturer has no insight into the original order from Airline ABC, and may not even know that his parts are going into the aircraft. Nor does he know anything about XYZ's production plan. The result is waste on a large scale.

4.34 This example is a gross simplification of reality. However, its premise is very real and the Forrester effect can be seen in supply chains in almost every industry. Sharing demand forecasts and production plans with suppliers reduces this effect.

Bottleneck items

4.35 Some stock items may be critical to the smooth running of the organisation and its operations, even though their usage value is not high. These would probably be classed as Category C items using ABC analysis. Their criticality, however, means that they must be available and they are sometimes described as **bottleneck** items. Strategies must be devised to ensure that such items are always available when required.

4.36 One method of dealing with such items would be to hold large amounts of stock As we have already seen, the cost of this would be a small price to pay when compared to the costs of disruption arising in the case of a stockout.

4.37 Another method that could be used might be **virtual inventory**. This is sometimes known as **bank inventory** because it is a system whereby groups of users may share common spare parts through a central 'bank'. The principle is based upon the assumption that, although parts may be required at short notice, they are unlikely to be needed by more than a few bank members at any one time.

4.38 The term 'bank' comes from the fact that banks never hold enough cash to satisfy all of their customers' requirements at any one time, but they do hold enough to cover a forecast 'spread' of customer requirements. This system does, however, require collaboration with other users of the items, some of whom could be competitors.

4.39 **Preventive maintenance** would also be a possible solution to the 'bottleneck' problem. This is where (usually) equipment such as cars or trains have vital components replaced on a regular basis even though they may not have reached the end of their useful life.

Seasonal demand

4.40 **Seasonality** is something else we need to consider in terms of ensuring that we have adequate stocks for the organisation's needs. Seasonality refers to the fact that, in some organisations, demand for items varies with the time of year. If there is a history of this for a certain item, there would at least be some past data upon which forecasts could be made.

Communication with internal customers

4.41 As you may have gathered, one of the most important factors in accurate demand forecasting is the quality of communication between stores (or inventory management) and other functions in the organisation – including stores' 'internal customers': the functions in the organisation that use the stock and information it provides. Effective communication is also important for co-ordination, planning and control, joint problem-solving, project working and the maintenance of co-operative relationships.

4.42 Stores and inventory managers will have to communicate regularly with functions such as:

- *Finance* – on areas such as budgeted expenditure, cost reduction targets, stock valuations and so on
- *Production* – on areas such as forecast and actual stock usage rates
- *Purchasing* – on areas such as supplier lead times and delivery performance record, order quantities
- *Marketing* – on areas such as forecast market demand.

4.43 Effective cross-functional communication with these important internal stakeholders may be achieved by mechanisms such as: regular briefing, information exchange and problem-solving meetings with internal customers; the use of questionnaires from stores to other functions, asking for feedback on how stores could improve its service; integrated information systems for data sharing; the use of intranet systems for internal messaging; joint education and training initiatives (for a shared understanding of issues); the inclusion of representatives of different functions on project teams, quality or service circles, or continuous improvement discussion groups and so on.

Summary: factors influencing demand forecasting

4.44 A number of factors might therefore influence demand forecasts, depending on the nature of the market, and the systems used by the organisation.

- Objective data: historical usage patterns and data (eg from internal operational records) and data supplied by other stakeholders (eg distributors or customers' EPOS systems)
- Subjective data: eg market research and opinion-based analysis of trends and environmental factors

- The bullwhip effect and other ways by which demand forecasts become 'amplified' as they are passed up the supply chain
- Seasonal or cyclical variations in demand (eg due to seasonal buying, the seasonality of the product, business cycles – boom and recession – and so on)
- Trends (or specific changes) in consumer demographics and behaviour, technology development, market prices, competitor activity and other environmental factors affecting demand

4.45 A number of factors will also impact on the *accuracy* of demand forecasting:

- The availability of past demand and usage data from which to extrapolate trends
- The validity and reliability of research and forecasting methodologies
- The skill and objectivity of forecasters
- The degree of change and unpredictability in the market and wider environment
- The accuracy of available information, and the quality of information sharing and communication with suppliers and customers (eg minimising potential for the bullwhip effect).

Chapter summary

- Stock control and replenishment involve ensuring that we have enough stock (without overstocking), as well as triggering the ordering process for new deliveries when we realise that we are running out of stock.
- If demand and/or usage of items is steady and predictable, stock control is relatively straightforward.
- Buffer stocks are stocks held just in case demand suddenly and unpredictably increases.
- In a periodic review system, the stock level of an item is examined on a periodic (fixed time interval) basis and a replenishment order is placed to top up stock to the desired level.
- In a fixed order quantity system, stock is replenished with a predetermined (fixed order) quantity when inventory falls to the predetermined reorder level.
- The economic order quantity is the optimum quantity of stock to reorder in a fixed order quantity system, so as to minimise the total of holding costs and acquisition costs.
- Forecasting demand is an important part of stock control. Techniques such as simple moving average and weighted average can help with this. Subjective methods (such as the Delphi method) may also be used.
- The Forrester effect suggests that, in traditional supply chains, a small change in final consumer demand leads to a much bigger change in demand 'upstream' in the supply chain.

 Self-test questions

Numbers in brackets refer to the paragraphs above where your answers can be checked.

1   What are the main purposes of stock control and replenishment? (1.1, 1.4)

2   Distinguish between demand and usage. (1.5.)

3   What is meant by buffer stocks? (1.9)

4   Distinguish between periodic review systems and fixed order quantity systems. (2.1)

5   List advantages and disadvantages of (a) periodic review systems and (b) fixed order quantity systems. (Tables 4.2 and 4.3)

6   Give a formula for calculating EOQ. (3.2)

7   What sources of information might be used in forecasting demand for a stock item? (4.4)

8   Distinguish between simple moving average and weighted average in the context of demand forecasting. (4.12)

9   Explain two types of trend that might be used in the 'trend analysis' method of forecasting. (4.16)

10   Explain the bullwhip effect. (4.29ff)

CHAPTER 5

Warehouse Location

Assessment criteria and indicative content

2.1 Describe the principles of stores and warehouse design

- Location of stores and warehouses

Section headings

1 Transport, accessibility and functionality
2 Size and flexibility of premises
3 Cost issues in warehouse location
4 External factors affecting warehouse location

1   Transport, accessibility and functionality

Introduction

1.1 A warehouse (or store) may be defined as a facility providing for the efficient handling and storage of goods and materials in a planned space environment.

1.2 The location of the warehouse is an important part of the process of materials handling. In this respect, we need an overall view of the whole supply chain because, unless the warehouse is located well, it will significantly increase the costs of our supplies and the cost of our products. This, in turn, might have an effect on our customers' loyalty and the success of our company.

1.3 The location of the warehouse is important because it should be able to add value to the supply chain. When we select a warehouse site we will commit our company to a service and cost structure for a long time; if we make an error it may reduce the competitiveness of our company.

1.4 Here are some of the factors that affect our choice of warehouse location.

- Proximity of our suppliers and customers
- Availability of existing premises or land
- Costs of establishing new facilities
- Road network proximity
- Road-rail terminals proximity
- Availability of human resources and skill base
- Environmental issues
- Types of goods being moved, for example, perishable or hazardous goods
- Local and regional planning considerations and government incentives such as the availability of development grants

1.5 Our choice of location must satisfy some conflicting demands. We need adequate speed of response for customer satisfaction and yet we must be close enough to our suppliers to reduce transportation costs. We should also relate the location of the warehouse to the business plan which tells us where the organisation will be in 5–10 years' time. We should include factors such as the quantity and type of product we are likely to hold, our potential customer base and also any future research and development issues the plan may highlight.

Strategic issues in warehouse locations and facilities

1.6 The first question that needs to be answered here is 'do we need a warehouse?' Many organisations are moving towards just in time processes. Operating without a warehouse can greatly reduce overhead costs and this can lead to the organisation being more 'lean' and competitive.

1.7 It is worth remembering that many items can be stored in a **stockyard**. These are open storage areas often located next to a warehouse and are most often used for the storage of non-perishable goods. The use of stockyards, whilst not usually eliminating the need for a warehouse, can affect the size of warehouse needed. This could have a 'knock-on' effect on the warehouse location.

1.8 If we decide that we do need a warehouse, we need to decide how many warehouses will be required to serve both internal and external customers. Another question is whether to centralise or decentralise stocks. A centralised warehouse system will have relatively low warehousing costs and high transport costs. A decentralised system will be the reverse of this.

1.9 In order to make a decision here, a full comparison of storage and transportation costs should be made. This is illustrated in Figure 5.1. The optimum number of warehouses can be chosen by comparing the relationship between the number of warehouses and the total distribution costs. Note that storage costs increase steadily as we increase the number of warehouses; whereas transport costs reduce, because a higher number of warehouses means greater proximity to customers and suppliers and hence reduced distances travelled.

Figure 5.1 *The costs of warehousing*

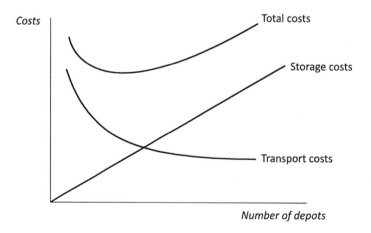

Transport and accessibility

1.10 Total transport costs vary from single to multiple distribution centres in proportion to two main cost elements.

- Long distance bulk trunking (primary transport)
- Local frequent deliveries (secondary transport)

1.11 After considering the broad strategic criteria there are usually three general solutions (although other combinations may develop or evolve to suit certain organisations).

- The central store, distribution centre, factory warehouse
- Warehouse plus regional distribution centres (RDCs)
- RDCs plus decentralised local unitary centres

1.12 Optimum location analysis for storage and warehouse facilities should be considered a key strategic issue. The warehouse and its storage capability and capacity are fundamental issues and are matters which should be under regular review. The value of a store should be viewed in the service value terms it provides. The trade-off is in establishing and managing warehouse costs against the service level provided by the store. This concept of value of service is sometimes difficult to quantify.

1.13 It is worth remembering the basic principles in both distribution and stores management which are that the costs incurred in the process of storing, handling and moving goods add cost but not value to the unit items. That is not to say that the added cost does not provide value to an organisation in availability or service level aspects, but the intrinsic value of the unit does not increase. Equally, the less space that can be assigned to warehouses, the more capital may be available for added-value production space in a factory.

1.14 There is a balance to be struck in terms of service level for a business. Here are some of the strategic and organisational factors that influence the decision.

- The dynamics of the market being served
- The form, volume and type of goods to be stored
- The company strategic policy and goals on customer service and warehouse costs
- The options available on transport network infrastructure and modal transport choices available
- Third-party or specialist distribution services available as an alternative to in-house operations

1.15 The decision on what type of distribution service and what number of warehouses is needed will depend to some extent on the type of transport system to be used. There follows a brief description of the main modes of transport that are available.

1.16 **Road transport**. The main advantages of transporting materials via road are flexibility, accessibility and cost.

- **Flexibility** – delivery or collection can be made between any number of points served by the road without the need for special terminals.
- **Accessibility** – even the most remote centres can be supplied. Road networks have improved and many cities can be reached within a few hours with trucking generally carried out overnight when the roads are quieter.
- **Cost** – distribution costs can be kept down by optimisation of contract arrangements, consolidation of loads and by carrying return loads.

1.17 The main disadvantages of road transport are infrastructure problems, environmental concerns – and, again, cost.

- **Infrastructure problems** – poor road conditions especially in less developed countries can cause delays.
- **Environmental concerns** – ever increasing levels of traffic have an impact on environmental pollution.
- **Cost** – road can sometimes be an expensive mode for large volumes of small consignments.

1.18   **Rail transport**: The main advantages of rail transport are flexibility of load, flexibility of service and warehousing and storage facilities.

- **Flexibility of load** – almost anything can be transported by rail with charges negotiated along commercial lines
- **Flexibility of service** – normal freight, fast freight, etc
- **Warehousing** and storage facilities and private sidings can be offered for the convenience of the purchaser.

1.19   The main disadvantages are distance, timing and vulnerability.

- **Distance** – the final point of delivery is often distant from the main line.
- **Timing** – deliveries for specific dates cannot always be guaranteed.
- **Vulnerability** – strong packaging may be required for journeys to avoid deterioration or contamination from other products, etc.

1.20   **Air transport**. The main advantages of this process are speed, reduced packaging costs, insurance costs, reliability and location.

- **Speed** – air transport is by far the quickest method, at least in international trade.
- **Reduced packaging costs** – lighter packaging is acceptable.
- **Insurance costs** by air are generally cheaper than freight insurance, owing to higher security levels.
- **Reliability** – deliveries can now more easily be guaranteed.
- **Location** – airports are located close to major cities.

1.21   The main disadvantages are: **bureaucracy** (the gains in speed by air are often offset by delays in transport from air terminals), **size limitation** of packaging, and **environmental factors** (air transport can be affected by adverse weather conditions).

1.22   **Water transport**. This covers both sea and inland waterways. The main advantage of this system is **cost** (it is cheaper to transport large or heavy items long distances via water and it is therefore a good mode for transporting items such as oil, coal or cars). Sea transport can be chartered or organised using scheduled routes. The main disadvantages are that **packaging** must be very strong to allow for adverse weather conditions; **speed** is very slow and **onward delivery** to the customer will need to be supported by other modes of transport; **insurance costs** can be high owing to deterioration factors and delay caused by weather conditions.

1.23   Much transport is carried out by road and many organisations have distribution centres as near as possible to motorway networks and junctions. Additionally, there are some large industrial estates situated near to major motorway junctions that cater for distribution 'hubs'.

1.24   If rail transport is to be used extensively, the warehouse should be located as near as possible to rail links. Some large organisations that use rail transport have sidings on their premises. However, if any transport mode is to be used extensively, other than road transport, access to appropriate freight hubs is essential.

1.25   **Accessibility** of potential locations should be taken into account at all times. The quality of local roads will determine, to a great extent, the ability of large vehicles to access the site. Factors such as bottlenecks must also be taken into account because delays so caused can add to costs. Also, such factors as congestion charges and restrictions on freight movement at certain times imposed by local authorities need consideration.

1.26 We need to view the issue of the warehouse site as a whole. Rarely does any site match our ideal requirements so we must decide our priorities and make trade-offs between functions at the planning stage. Other considerations may be as follows.

- Type, size and number of products stored, including external storage
- Site access to transport networks
- Type of trucks and manoeuvring areas
- Environmental and local authority constraints
- Employee car parking

Functionality

1.27 Lastly, in this part of the chapter, **functionality** (how well does the warehouse satisfy the organisation's storage requirements) needs brief consideration. Potential locations for a warehouse must be suitable and cover all the requirements mentioned above as far as possible. Considerations as to whether the building should be single-storey or multi-storey need to be made. We will consider this factor later in this chapter.

1.28 Also, we need to consider whether items to be stored will have special storage requirements. Some items must be stored under special conditions (eg freezer stores; low humidity; etc). Such requirements will need to be catered for and might affect the choice of warehouse location. Other materials (such as explosive or flammable ones) should be stored as far away as possible from other buildings and residential areas.

1.29 The variety of function and purpose can be considerable and different companies will use warehouses in different ways. Warehouses can fulfil a wide variety of roles.

- To act as a collection and distribution point for items of stock
- To provide convenient and secure storage for items of value
- To provide space for related administrative activities, such as stores issue and offices
- To house materials handling equipment
- To keep down production costs by allowing long production runs
- To help link demand requirements with production capabilities
- To provide a buffer to smooth variations between supply and demand
- To enable procurement savings through large volume purchases
- To enable large seasonal demands to be catered for more economically
- To provide a good customer service
- To allow cost trade-offs with the transport system
- To facilitate order assembly
- To provide a wide range of products from different suppliers in one location
- To cover for production shutdowns

1.30 Properly designed, planned, organised and managed a warehouse can offer higher levels of service with lower inventory and lower costs. Correct location, good design, appropriate and practical use of stock location systems and, often, increasing size can make the warehouse a distribution centre rather than merely a stores area. Properly utilised warehouses can enhance customer service and add value to the product.

2 Size and flexibility of premises

Introduction

2.1 The size of accommodation required will depend upon the extent of stockholding required. It will also depend upon the bulk and nature of the goods bought in, and variations in sales turnover. Changes in accommodation required may be indicated by the sales production budget for the next period. The value of sales turnover is not a good guide except in a comparative sense, because the materials stored may be small and expensive (jewels or gold, to take extreme examples) or bulky and cheap (such as paving stones).

2.2 Most forward-looking firms will wish to allow for expansion in all sections of the business, and provision must be made for possible increases in stockholding. This type of consideration might be 'on hold' in many organisations owing to the economic downturn since 2008/09 but would normally be regarded as being important.

2.3 Organisations with strategic objectives and projections of growth and increased sales volume must carry out long-term projections of future activity levels. Wherever possible, the location and premises chosen or constructed should have scope for future expansion. It might be useful to consider locating or constructing premises with parts that could be sold off or used for other purposes if the organisation's market shrinks.

2.4 The cost of providing storage accommodation may possibly be a limiting factor, in that this must be kept within economic bounds, and within the budget available for this aspect of the business. In general, the storage conditions must be just good enough to prevent the mishaps which can befall stored materials. However, care must be taken because it would be disruptive and costly to relocate after, say, three years because of insufficient warehouse capacity.

Proximity to operational premises and customer sites

2.5 Firstly, we will consider **factory warehouses** – in other words, warehouses that serve other parts of a factory (usually the production department). Here the warehouse should be sited as close as possible to those departments that use its services most. The closeness will preferably be in the horizontal plane rather than in the vertical but in multi-storey buildings the stores department may be sited on the ground floor, serving production floors above by means of a lift.

2.6 The important point to note is that stored materials should be transported as little as possible before they are used. Handling costs, human and/or mechanical, should be kept as low as possible. Additionally, the shorter the distance between production shop and stores department, the less chance there is of people becoming 'lost' for short periods whilst on their way to hand in requisitions.

2.7 The siting of the stores department must be planned, as far as possible, as part of the layout for the departments served. If a new factory site is being planned, a work study team may assist the architect in the siting of interdependent departments. Usually the stores department will flank one outside wall of the factory building, to facilitate loading and unloading of vehicles.

2.8 **Distribution warehouses** are warehouses that serve either a number of retail outlets or a number of user departments or factory sites, often over a wide area. Examples of these would be the regional distribution centres that many supermarket chains have developed.

2.9 In this type of environment, transport is one of the largest cost elements. One of the best ways of reducing this is to locate the distribution centre as near as possible to the point(s) of demand. This can only be effectively achieved by means of accurate forecasting of demand patterns and will require close liaison with the sales and marketing functions. This forecasting of demand can only provide the region or area of the country where the distribution centre(s) should be located.

3 Cost issues in warehouse location

Buy or lease?

3.1 Warehouses, potentially, are extremely expensive. A new, purpose-built warehouse, particularly if it is large, would have a very high cost. There would be the cost of the land, the cost of building materials and the cost of personnel required to build it. There would also be the profit margin of the building company.

3.2 On the other hand, if an existing warehouse is purchased, there may still be a potentially high cost, particularly if the warehouse is large. In both of these situations, the costs would increase if the warehouse were in a part of the country where land and property is expensive. In fact, organisations would be more likely to have a warehouse away from such areas but with good transport links. Given the expense of purchasing or building a warehouse, it is not surprising that some organisations consider leasing premises instead.

3.3 However, there are advantages to purchasing a warehouse, whether purpose-built or already existing. Firstly, it would be an appreciating investment (assuming increasing property prices) and would be an asset of the organisation. Outright ownership also has an advantage over leasing in that it allows the owner independence and control in terms of how the warehouse is used and operated. This is because, provided local laws on planning permission are not flouted, the warehouse owner may do whatever he likes with it.

3.4 On the other hand, leasing a warehouse has an advantage over purchasing if funds are limited or the costs of finance are high to the point of being prohibitive. It can also be argued that leasing can be more flexible. This is because, after a time, the organisation might decide it needs a different type of warehouse because its needs have changed. In this situation, it would be much easier to return the existing warehouse to its owner and look to find another one to lease that would be more suitable to the new requirements. This would also be much quicker to arrange than purchasing a new warehouse.

Purpose-built or adapt existing premises?

3.5 This is a decision that might have to be made when considering buying a new warehouse (adapting leased property is unlikely to be possible). It is likely that adapting property would be cheaper in the short term. However, the potential for adaptation is likely to be limited, particularly over time. Therefore, purchasing a purpose-built warehouse might be the better option. Whilst it is likely to be more expensive in the short term, it would have the advantage of being able to be tailored to suit the exact needs of the organisation.

3.6 Carter and Price (in *Integrated Materials Management*) cite a number of pros and cons relating to purpose built stores and converted stores: Table 5.1.

Table 5.1 *Purpose-built vs converted stores buildings*

PURPOSE-BUILT BUILDINGS	CONVERTED BUILDINGS
Advantages • Most efficient layout can be planned • Latest techniques can be incorporated • Building is exactly adapted to the firm's needs	*Disadvantages* • Layout may be tricky (eg with uneven floors and badly placed doors) • Expensive equipment may be needed to correct environmental conditions • Not exactly adapted to the firm's needs
Disadvantages • Design and construction is expensive • Conflicting interests between stores and other functions such as finance • Risk of expensive misjudgment	*Advantages* • Inexpensive compared with construction from scratch • Flexibility – if needs change, stock can be moved elsewhere • Careful planning and layout can produce very useful storage facilities

4   External factors affecting warehouse location

Local labour force and infrastructure

4.1   However an organisation acquires a warehouse (buying or leasing, see above), it will require labour to operate it. Many warehouses, with the exception of highly mechanised ones using automated guidance vehicles and computer controlled mobile racking, are labour-intensive. This means that when it is planned to build or purchase/lease a warehouse, the availability of labour in the locality must be considered.

4.2   It is possible that some staff would need to be skilled or semi-skilled. Here, a decision would be needed on whether to recruit unskilled staff and train them or to recruit skilled and semi-skilled labour from the surrounding area. The decision here might depend on the availability of suitable staff in the locality of the warehouse.

4.3   In terms of the cost of labour, it will be harder to attract staff in areas where there is full employment. Also, average wages in such an area would be high and would need to be matched or exceeded in order to attract staff.

4.4   In terms of **local infrastructure**, research has been carried out and the following findings are widely accepted. These concern employers' and employees' preferences regarding where a warehouse is located and relates to what both parties want in a warehouse's location.

4.5   An employer's preferences are as follows.

- Quality of workforce (the most important preference)
- Access to the national road network
- Low overhead costs
- Quality of the local environment
- Local economic conditions
- Competitive wage levels.

4.6 Employees' preferences are as follows.

- Proximity to public transport (presumably for getting to and from work)
- The warehouse to be in a safe area
- The warehouse to be near to shops
- Proximity of cafés, pubs and restaurants

Political influences on warehouse location

4.7 The first of these to consider is **grants and regional aid**. Over time, many regions have given grants to businesses that wished to set up in their region. This was done as an incentive to encourage businesses to the region in order to improve employment in the region or to enhance the region's image. Such grants are still available and if an organisation needs to establish a warehouse, it would be worth checking with the various local authorities in the desired region.

4.8 There has been some targeting of regions for 'rejuvenation' and regional grants may be available to encourage businesses to set up in particular regions. The only problem here is that warehouses are not always as attractive to regions as are (for example) manufacturing companies because they tend not to employ as many people. In any regional rejuvenation project, encouraging employment is a prime consideration.

Environmental factors and local lobby groups

4.9 It is possible that local residents may object to the establishment of a warehouse in their area. They may cite environmental reasons for such objections. Although warehouses generally do not create much, if any, environmental pollution, they can add to traffic congestion and noise pollution. This is particularly true if the warehouse is a large distribution warehouse which has lorries and vans entering and leaving it almost constantly.

4.10 All of the above is particularly true when a warehouse is located in a primarily residential area. This gives rise to possible danger posed by lorries to pedestrians, particularly children. This might lead to residents' pressure groups applying pressure to local politicians to prohibit the establishment of a warehouse. Such pressure groups would consist of voters who could exert pressure on local politicians. If the warehouse establishment continued in a manner that ignored local concerns it could damage the organisation's image and attract negative publicity.

4.11 If such situations arise it would be useful to understand the concerns of local pressure groups. It is also a good idea to be prepared to negotiate with such groups to show that your organisation wishes to have a positive impact on the locality. This might mean that your organisation would need to compromise on some activities such as establishing preferred routes for vehicles arriving from suppliers or leaving to travel to customers. These routes might avoid residential roads and streets as much as possible and would need to be communicated to users of the warehouse. It would be particularly important to ensure that third party transport providers were aware of such arrangements.

Chapter summary

- It is important to ensure that a warehouse is suitably located. If not, the cost of supplies is likely to be higher than necessary and our ability to supply customers will be impaired.
- Warehouse site selection will commit our company to a service and cost structure and if we get it wrong it may reduce the competitiveness of our company.
- There is a long list of considerations that contribute to our warehouse location decision. Some of these may conflict with each other such as: proximity of our suppliers and customers and availability of existing premises or land.
- The first decision to be made is whether we need a warehouse. If we decide that we do, we then need to decide how many warehouses we need.
- We must ensure that our choice of warehouse(s) gives us the lowest possible total distribution cost, which involves balancing the costs of stores and transport against the service we want to provide to the business.
- The decision as to what type of distribution service and the number of warehouses required will depend on the type of transport system to be used (road, rail, etc).
- The size of accommodation required will depend upon the extent of stockholding required and the bulk and nature of the goods being used.
- When designing or acquiring a warehouse, provision should be made for possible expansion of the business and a subsequent increase in stockholding.
- Warehouses serving factories (production line requirements etc) should be sited as near to the factory and its production units as possible.
- Distribution warehouses should be sited as close as possible to the centres of demand for the products being stored.
- Decisions would need to be made as to whether a new, purpose built, warehouse would be a better proposition than acquiring one that already exists. The relative costs and advantages and disadvantages of each would have to be compared.
- A decision would also need to be made as to whether purchasing a warehouse would be better than leasing one.
- When acquiring a warehouse the availability of suitable labour in its area would need to be considered owing to the fact that warehouse operation tends to be labour-intensive.
- Employers have preferences regarding warehouse location as do employees. These should both be taken into account when considering moving an existing warehouse facility to a new location.
- Grants may be available to assist the establishment of a warehouse in particular regions.
- The effect on the local environment must be considered when making a decision as to where to locate a warehouse. These effects are usually such things as noise pollution, traffic congestion and possible danger to pedestrians posed by lorries.

Self-test questions

Numbers in brackets refer to the paragraphs above where your answers can be checked.

1   What is the likely consequence of an organisation not locating a warehouse appropriately? (1.3)

2   Give four factors that might affect an organisation's choice of warehouse location. (1.4)

3   What is a stockyard and how might it affect the choice of warehouse an organisation might make? (1.7)

4   Give examples of special storage requirements. (1.28)

5   What is the size of a warehouse likely to depend upon? (2.1)

6   What would be the main considerations in deciding where to locate a 'factory warehouse'? (2.5, 2.6)

7   Describe and give an example of a distribution warehouse. (2.8)

8   What advantages might purchasing a warehouse have over leasing one? (3.3)

9   What advantages might leasing a warehouse have? (3.4)

10   Give one advantage and one disadvantage of having a purpose-built warehouse. (Table 5.1)

11   Give three likely employer's preferences that might affect the choice of location for a warehouse. (4.5)

12   Explain how grants from local or regional authorities might affect the choice of warehouse location. (4.7, 4.8)

13   Explain how an organisation might try to take steps to reduce local residents' fears regarding a warehouse being located in their locality. (4.11)

CHAPTER 6

Stores and Warehouse Design

Assessment criteria and indicative content

2.1 Describe the principles of stores and warehouse design

- Stores and warehouse design
- Factors that influence stores and warehouse layout
- Flow, space utilisation and flexibility

Section headings

1. Principles of warehouse design
2. Factors influencing warehouse layout
3. Positioning stock in the warehouse
4. Flow of goods through the warehouse

1 Principles of warehouse design

Introduction

1.1 A warehouse needs to be designed (or adapted) to meet our needs. To this end, there are a number of considerations that should be taken into account.

1.2 The overriding consideration is that the design and layout of the warehouse must meet our needs. In other words, the design must be suitable for the items that we will hold in stock. It must also suit the facilities we use to hold the items (racking, etc) and the materials handling equipment we use to move the items around (forklift trucks etc).

1.3 In summary, the principles we need to consider in terms of design are as follows.

- Space
- Structure
- Environment

Space

1.4 In any warehouse, items will arrive, be put away on racking, in containers etc, and be despatched to users or customers. The overriding factor, therefore, in the design of a warehouse is that it must be large enough to cope with this throughput.

1.5 We can calculate the basic size requirements of the warehouse by forecasting demand for the items we will stock. This will provide an estimate of how much material will need to be stocked. From this, the space needed can be estimated. To this can be added estimates of how much space we will require for the racking we will need to store the items. Other factors will be the space needed for aisles for the materials handling equipment and the space needed for receiving and despatch areas.

1.6   In addition to the actual storage requirements it will be necessary to ensure that there is space for staff facilities. These will include offices and toilets as well as canteens and rest and relaxation areas.

1.7   Assuming we will need materials handling equipment to move goods around the warehouse, we will need to assess what types are needed. When this decision has been made, we can establish the size of aisles that will be needed for this equipment. An example here would be that, if forklift trucks are used, aisles need to be wide enough for the trucks to travel in and manoeuvre. There should also be no obstacles, such as pillars, that might impede their progress.

1.8   The warehouse will also need suitable goods receiving and despatch areas. Both of these will need adequate space for unloading goods (in the case of goods receiving) and for loading them (in the case of despatch). In both cases, there should be adequate space outside for lorries to be positioned for unloading and loading and to be parked whilst they wait their turn.

Structure

1.9   We are not concerned with detailed analysis of building techniques here but you should be aware that there is a choice whether to have a single-storey building or a multi-storey one. There is no 'correct' answer to this question: the building needs to have sufficient height to meet the organisation's needs. Both single-storey and multi-storey buildings have advantages.

1.10   Here are some advantages of single-storey buildings.

- The layout tends to be more flexible. There is a limit to the extent to which you can move things around multi-storey buildings owing to weight restrictions etc. This does not occur in single-storey buildings.
- The cost of building tends to be lower than that of multi-storey buildings.
- Materials handling costs are usually lower than those of multi-storey buildings because moving forklift trucks (for example) up and down between storeys would require extremely robust and costly equipment.

1.11   And here are some advantages of multi-storey buildings.

- The overall 'area' of the building (sometimes known as 'footprint') on the land is smaller than with singe-storey buildings.
- They will tend to have greater storage capacity because the total storage floor area will tend to be greater than with single-storey buildings.
- There should be less heat loss because of better insulation between floors.

1.12   Whilst multi-storey buildings do have advantages, and a multi-storey warehouse is most useful if linked to a multi-storey operations building, the general preference tends to be for single-storey warehouses. This does depend principally on the amount of land available to the organisation, however.

1.13   Other structural aspects of warehouse buildings include the following.

- Doors should be large enough to allow access – remember that forklift trucks, especially when loaded, can be very large – whilst at the same time providing adequate security.
- Windows, also, should be able to give adequate security.
- Floors should be hard-wearing and level (materials handling equipment can be very unstable if floors are not truly level).
- Walls should be robust.

1.14 Additionally, compliance with building regulations will be necessary. Also, if expansion of any kind is contemplated, planning regulations should be checked. It would also be worthwhile to check whether planning permission for any modifications and/or improvements would be available.

The working environment

1.15 Structural considerations are relevant also in designing the working environment. Here are some of the factors that must be addressed.

- Adequate lighting must be provided and, where possible, natural daylight (via skylights and large windows) should be used. A problem here, however, is the 'trade-off' between natural daylight and security.
- Good ventilation is necessary. Some warehouses might need particularly dry areas in order to store items that would be susceptible to damp. If this is the case, suitable equipment would be needed to maintain a dry environment.
- There should be adequate and unobtrusive heating equipment and insulation against heat loss and drafts should be considered.
- Essential safety equipment should be available as should access to such things as water for fire hoses.

2 Factors influencing warehouse layout

Preliminary considerations

2.1 Designing the layout of a warehouse involves a number of stages starting with a clear understanding of:

- The purpose of the warehouse
- The operations it will fulfil
- The anticipated volume and nature of work that will be undertaken.

2.2 From this understanding a simulated design can start to take shape. An 'ideal' layout can be planned; this will be adapted to a more realistic layout over time. Ergonomic methods can be used to ensure the layout minimises movement of goods and people.

2.3 As the design progresses, management and staff must be able to put forward their views and be given the opportunity to contribute to the new layout. Involvement of all relevant management and staff at an early stage is important and demonstrates good application of change management. Early involvement of external bodies (eg planning authority, local fire officer and insurance company) is also advisable.

2.4 The warehouse and its layout must meet specified requirements as well as taking account of possible business growth. The accuracy and completeness of the data on which any design is based will affect how well the final design reflects this. Much of this data can be gathered from the warehouse's IT systems relating to stock control and replenishment. IT systems can also be used to forecast future requirements.

2.5 Data required to develop the project will cover:

- Goods handled (inventory levels, handling requirements)
- Order characteristics (service levels, order frequency)
- Goods arrival and despatch patterns (vehicle types and sizes, unit loads to be handled)
- Warehouse operations (picking and packing, administration)

Design and layout principles

2.6   The most commonly accepted design and layout principles are as follows.

- Use a single-storey building wherever possible, as was suggested earlier. It is cheaper to construct, cost-effective and can allow for a design that maximises the cubic capacity of the warehouse.
- Use straight-line or 'throughflow' (see later in this chapter) of goods in and out of the warehouse with goods being delivered at one end, held, and ranked according to ABC analysis. They should be easily accessible for selection, packing and preparation for shipping and despatch. In reality this is not always attainable but the main consideration is that goods can 'flow' through the warehouse causing minimum disruption while remaining accessible.
- Utilise an effective storage plan to maximise warehouse operations and to avoid inefficiencies. Racking should be designed (if being built from scratch) or selected (if being purchased) to maximise the cubic capacity of the warehouse but should also take account of dedicated security areas, fire regulations (particularly emergency exit doors) and order preparation areas.
- To maximise efficiency the right storage and handling equipment must be used.
- Minimise aisle space within the constraints of the size, type and turning circle of materials handling equipment; consider also the products handled and the constraints they impose.
- Maximise use of the building's height to use the cubic capacity fully. Materials handling equipment and storage equipment such as racking should be selected to support this.

2.7   Warehouses will require an order preparation area where goods can be sorted or collated for despatch. This area will see considerable physical movement from the staff and good ergonomic design is essential to maximise productivity. Utilising cubic capacity in this area is difficult because of the need to keep orders within pickers' reach.

2.8   The warehouse layout and its objectives of **protection** and **efficiency** provide a good framework for determining the use of warehouse space. From a **protection** perspective:

- Space utilisation should separate hazardous materials from other items to reduce the risks involved.
- Items requiring special security should be located in a specific and protected area.
- Items requiring physical control such as refrigeration should have a dedicated area.
- Warehouse personnel should be made aware of the dangers of stacking light or fragile items near others that could cause them damage.

2.9   **Efficiency** has two aspects.

- Effective utilisation of space in the warehouse
- Placement of stock so as to minimise labour and handling costs

2.10   Faster-moving items should be in the most accessible areas. Size can also affect efficiency. Many companies store large items near the despatch area so as to minimise their handling. If the load size is large compared with the order size, storing the items close to the despatch area may again minimise handling costs.

2.11   Accessibility is therefore an important consideration in site layout. Vehicles need easy access, as do staff and the emergency services. Barriers and gatehouses with separate access for cars and commercial vehicles often provide external security. There should be enough space to allow vehicles to manoeuvre safely and ideally the site should offer room for expansion.

Storage and movement of stocks

2.12 Within the warehouse the use of storage systems is a major consideration because of the space utilised, their effect on work flow and the costs involved. Warehouses cope with a wide variety of goods and materials and in consequence a wide range of storage equipment has been developed to meet these needs.

2.13 As we have seen, holding items in stock incurs costs without adding value to the organisation's activities. Thus, in the warehouse, we should always try to maximise **throughput**. This is the term used to describe the volume of items passing through the warehouse in a given time. This should be achieved with the minimum of costs such as those that might arise from double handling, damage to items, losses and delays. 'Double handling' is the term used to describe putting items in the wrong place and then having to move them to the right place.

2.14 The movement of items through a warehouse can be summarised as follows.

- The goods are received into the warehouse.
- The goods are placed (located) into their storage locations.
- The goods are selected for use or issue to another site or customer.
- The goods are taken to the despatch area and loaded onto suitable transport. If they have been selected for use on site, they will simply be handed to the user upon receipt of a stores requisition.

2.15 The choice of a suitable storage system will depend on a number of factors, all of which should be balanced with the cost involved.

- Type of goods handled
- Suitability of goods for unit loads (see later in this chapter)
- Effective utilisation of the 'cube' of the building, perhaps requiring high-aisle racking and hence appropriate handling equipment
- Accessibility, security considerations and safety of personnel

2.16 The effective storage capacity of the warehouse may be constrained by:

- the use of fixed locations for certain stock lines
- the application of ABC analysis classifying stock into high-usage, medium-usage or low-usage stock areas
- whether goods can be held at random locations.

2.17 Whichever application is deemed to be suitable the utilisation of warehouse capacity will always be less than 100 per cent as the movement of goods creates a space that then needs to be refilled. The aim is to consider the type of product being held and to ensure that waste (in this case unnecessary movement and double handling) is minimised.

2.18 Considerations relating to effective and efficient stock location can be the subject of computer-simulated modelling to ensure that the operational design of the warehouse maximises space availability in the majority of anticipated situations.

2.19 The positioning and type of racking is an important consideration. Racking, or shelving, as well as supporting handling equipment, must be designed or selected to meet the needs of the operation.

6

3 Positioning stock in the warehouse

General principles of positioning

3.1 Considerable thought should be given to where the racking will be located together with the usage of the goods held on that racking. As we have already seen, items should flow through the warehouse as quickly as possible. This means that inefficiencies such as unnecessary manoeuvring, turning, backtracking and double handling should be avoided as much as possible. We can achieve this by ensuring, where possible, that items move through the warehouse in a straight line.

3.2 It is worth mentioning that ABC analysis is often applied within warehouses to help in analysing the flow of work. Dividing goods held into A, B and C categories in terms of annual usage helps to formulate possible positions where stock should be located.

- High usage (Category A) items should be located close to entrances, despatch areas or pick-and-pack areas as deemed necessary.
- Medium usage (Category B) items will be located further from the main areas.
- Low usage (Category C) items will be kept in less utilised areas.

3.3 Sometimes referred to as 'popularity storage', this method can give maximum use of space with more effective speed of issue. Owing to the closeness of the appropriate goods less stress is placed on labour and equipment.

3.4 Other considerations that can help determine where items should be positioned are as follows.

- Similarity: if items that are similar in nature are stored together it will be easier for warehouse personnel to remember where they are positioned.
- Size or weight: the manual lifting of heavy items should be minimised. In fact, health and safety regulations place severe limits on this. Because of this, heavy items should not be stored high up and large and/or abnormally shaped items might be better stored in a stockyard or separate annex. This would improve the use of space in the warehouse as well as the throughflow of goods.
- Special characteristics: some items have special storage needs.

3.5 Here are some examples of this final point.

- Items that might be 'attractive', and therefore might be pilfered, should be stored in secure, lockable areas.
- Items such as fresh foodstuffs might need to be refrigerated.
- Flammable substances (or even explosives) will need to be stored well away from other stocks (often well away from the warehouse itself).
- In some warehouses, staff might have to put items together into 'kits'. In this case, it might be a good idea to store such items close together to facilitate the kit assembly.

Fixed-location storage

3.6 Fixed locations, where goods are in a strict sequence with commodity cataloguing or coding, are used where the commodity groups are well defined and the product range is stable. Fixed locations enable staff to become familiar with product positions, and this can be an advantage in certain types of operation (eg spares for the automotive industry). However, fixed locations restrict flexibility and changes to the item profiles can cause major upheaval.

3.7 Similarity, size, weight or the nature of goods (hazardous, refrigerated, etc) may also be considered when positioning stock. The aim is to minimise movement and double-handling while aiding the flow of goods and work through the warehouse.

3.8 Fixed location storage can make it easy for staff to remember where each item is, often by grouping related items together. Different product characteristics can be accommodated by different types of storage areas.

Random location storage

3.9 Random location, as the name suggests, involves putting incoming goods in storage in a random manner. If the warehouse handles standardised goods this method can offer optimisation of racking, allowing for high rates of warehouse fill. The system requires an excellent stock control and location system as goods are placed wherever is convenient.

3.10 Good IT systems are usually necessary in conjunction with random location. When goods arrive, the system can display a suitable location. 'Suitable' means a location that will cope satisfactorily with the size and nature of the items as well as whether they are fast-moving or not. When goods are required for despatch, the system can reveal where they are located. In anything but the smallest of warehouses random location would be impossible without a good IT system to monitor stock movement.

4   Flow of goods through the warehouse

Straight line (throughflow) system

4.1 Whether ABC analysis or another system more relevant to the needs of an individual organisation is used, it is important to have a smooth flow within a warehouse environment. Straight-line flows, 'U' flows and flows based around usage all follow a 'one way' system of movement that serves to reduce congestion and improve safety in the working warehouse environment.

4.2 **Straight line** or **throughflow** is one of the most effective layouts, with goods arriving at one end of the warehouse and being handled in a designated receiving area before being located in their appropriate position in the warehouse. Issuing and despatch takes place at the other end of the building. Materials flow from one end of the building to the other in a straight line without corners and bends becoming an issue.

Figure 6.1 *The throughflow system*

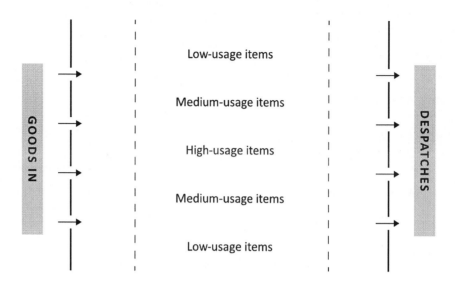

4.3 Advantages of the throughflow system

- Useful if goods in and goods out vehicle requirements are different.
- Works well if it is in a natural flow with other processes.
- Total separation of the 'in' and 'out' sections reduces scope for error.

4.4 Disadvantages of the throughflow system

- Loading bays (one at each end of the building) take up a lot of space.
- Bay security and management may be more difficult, again because the two bays are separated.
- Internal movement may be greater than with other systems (from one end of the building to the other).

U-shaped ('horseshoe') system

4.5 **U-shaped** or **horseshoe** flow will be considered when the receiving area and the issuing and despatch area are at the same end of the building. Goods simply flow from left (receiving) to right (issuing and despatch) in a horseshoe-flow pattern.

Figure 6.2 *The 'U' shaped flow system*

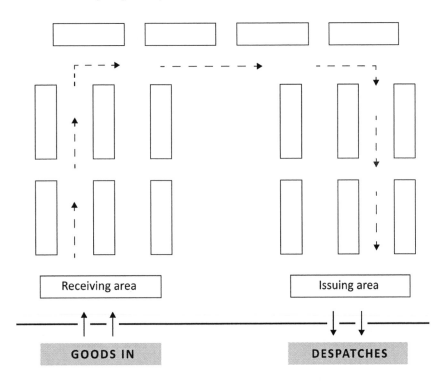

Inverted 'T' system

4.6   Inverted 'T' flow allows the warehouse to be divided to meet long-term storage needs. Stock is then positioned in line with usage, the most frequently used items being nearer the pick-and-pack or despatch area.

Figure 6.3 *The 'inverted T' system*

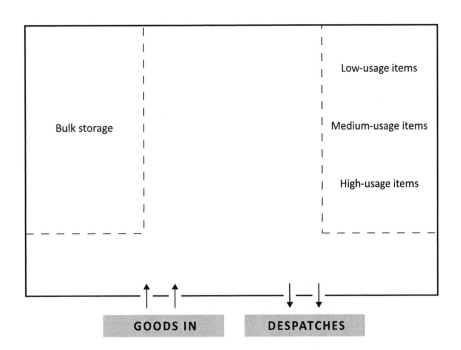

4.7 Advantages of the inverted 'T' flow system

- Good utilisation of loading bays and materials handling equipment
- Flexibility for expansion on three sides
- Popularity storage reduces need for movements
- Segregation aids handling

4.8 Disadvantages of the inverted 'T' flow system

- Central aisle becomes prone to congestion.
- Expansion requires some modification of flow.
- Moving items from bulk storage to stock or to despatch requires tight control.

Crossflow system

4.9 The crossflow layout utilises the full width of the warehouse. Within the low-usage, medium-usage and high-usage areas there is often a usage weighting placing; for example the most frequently used Category B items are placed towards the end of racking in their row to allow for easy access.

Figure 6.4 *The crossflow system*

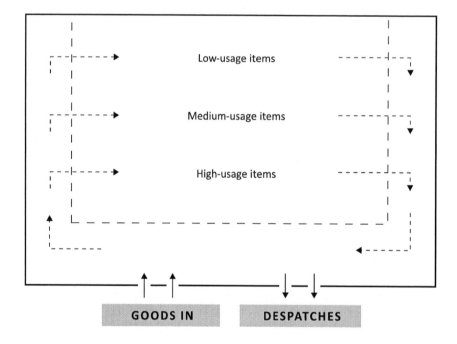

4.10 Advantages of the crossflow system

- Good utilisation of loading bays and materials handling equipment
- Flexibility for expansion on three sides
- Popularity storage reduces movement
- A combination of 'bulk' and 'standard' stock can be utilised across the width of the warehouse, normally with Category A items the most accessible and bulk items the least accessible in terms of flow
- One-way flow is clearly defined

4.11   Disadvantages of the 'crossflow' system

- Segregation into high, medium and low usage may not always be possible.
- Combination of 'bulk' and 'standard' stock can present problems.

Cornerflow system

4.12   In the **corner warehouse flow**, goods flow in and out of adjacent walls of the warehouse, joined at a corner. This layout serves to reduce congestion in the aisles particularly in terms of high throughput. The system often provides a practical operating compromise that allows the goods inwards, flow and despatch areas to integrate effectively.

Figure 6.5 *The cornerflow system*

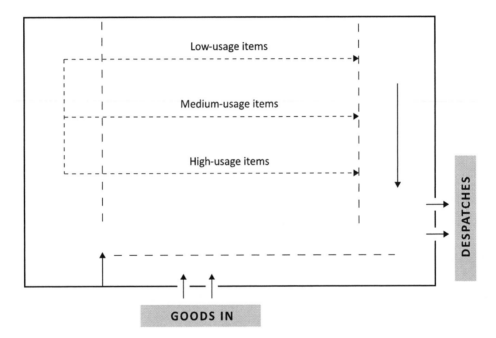

Using the cube

4.13   All warehousing systems are a compromise between efficient use of warehouse space and ready access to the goods. Warehouse design, the positioning and use of racking and the flow of goods and work through the warehouse are all closely interlinked and should be viewed as such when modelling or simulating the working of the warehouse.

4.14   In any warehouse, the total available space should be utilised where possible. This includes not just the length and breadth of the building but its height also. This principle is known as **using the cube**. The total height of the building can be incorporated into the available storage space by use of racking systems such as high-density racking or by the use of mezzanine floors.

4.15   Mezzanine floors are non-structural floors that can be placed inside the warehouse, usually attached to one wall of the building. They provide an extra storey between the building's floor and ceiling although they will not usually be suitable for heavy items. They can be useful for the storage of small, lightweight, items and/or an office.

Chapter summary

- The main considerations when designing a warehouse and its layout are: space; structure; environment.
- Any warehouse must be designed so that it can cope with the throughput of materials from goods inward to despatch.
- There should be enough space in a warehouse to contain all of the required racking and other storage equipment, materials handling equipment and offices.
- Warehouses can be single-storey or multi-storey but the advantages of single-storey buildings usually outweigh those of multi-storey buildings.
- The design and layout of a warehouse must cater for:
  — Goods handled (inventory levels, handling requirements);
  — Order characteristics (service levels, order frequency);
  — Goods arrival and despatch patterns (vehicle types and sizes, unit loads to be handled);
  — Warehouse operations (picking and packing, administration).
- The movement of items through a warehouse can be summarised as follows:
  — The goods are received into the warehouse
  — The goods are placed in their storage locations
  — The goods are selected for use or issue
  — The goods are taken to the despatch area
- The choice of a suitable storage system will depend on a number of factors.
  — Type of goods handled
  — Suitability of goods for unit loads
  — Effective utilisation of the 'cube' of the building,
  — Accessibility, security considerations and safety of personnel
- Using ABC analysis can help in deciding where to locate different items: the most frequently used are placed near to the despatch bay and less frequently used items are placed further away
- 'Fixed location' storage means that items are located in the same place all of the time. This helps personnel remember where different items can be found.
- 'Random location' storage means that items are located anywhere where there is a suitable space when they arrive in the warehouse. This represents a potentially large saving of space required.
- One of the most important aspects of warehouse design is the provision of 'flow' from when the goods arrive, are moved into the warehouse and later on, are despatched.
- There are many different types of 'flow' system: throughflow, 'U-shaped', inverted 'T', etc but all provide a system where movement in the warehouse is 'one-way'.

Self-test questions

Numbers in brackets refer to the paragraphs above where your answers can be checked.

1   What are the main principles we need to consider when designing a warehouse unit's layout? (1.3)

2   What factors need to be considered when designing a warehouse to ensure that we have one that will meet our needs? (1.4–1.8)

3   Apart from the question of single-storey or multi-storey buildings what other structural considerations need to be taken into account when designing a warehouse? (1.13)

4   Give three main principles of warehouse design and layout. (2.6)

5   Define 'throughput' of materials and state why it is important. (2.13)

6   Define 'ABC analysis' and explain how it can influence where items are located in the warehouse. (3.2, 3.3)

7   What are the advantages of the 'straight line' or 'throughflow' layout? (4.3)

8   What are the advantages of the 'crossflow' layout? (4.10)

6

CHAPTER 7

Product Coding

Assessment criteria and indicative content

 Describe the use of product coding in inventory operations

- Systems for product coding
- Barcoding
- Order tracking technologies
- The use of RFID technologies

Section headings

1 Types of coding system
2 Characteristics of a good coding system
3 Order tracking technologies

1   Types of coding system

Introduction

1.1 This chapter deals with some of the main methods of controlling and monitoring stocks on a daily basis. Coding systems are one of the chief ways by which a warehouse manager can be aware of what is in stock, in what quantity, where it is located and how it is moving in and out of the warehouse.

1.2 Within most organisations there will be a variety of goods stocked for the direct business and its support. Stock is classified into a number of general categories and is linked to various stages of purchasing, manufacturing, marketing and distribution processes. Large inventories cannot be managed without some logical, organised system of stock identification and coding. As a guide, Figure 7.1 shows some of the recognised advantages for organisations using an appropriate coding system.

Figure 7.1 *Advantages of a stock coding system*

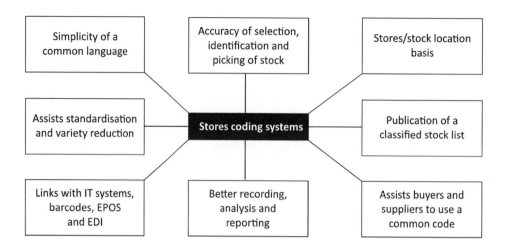

Numeric coding systems

1.3 There are many types of coding scheme: numeric, letters, colour, barcoding, coding by end use, coding by nature of the item, symbolic coding. There are also some variations and 'sub-types'. We shall consider each in turn.

1.4 Numeric codes are the most widely used system. The general class of the product is identified by an initial number with sub-categories as outlined below.

1.5 A **sequential coding system** allocates numbers in sequence without any attempt to relate them to specific items in a structured way. This method is particularly useful when it is difficult to predict the range to be covered by the coding scheme. As this makes it very difficult for people to recognise an item simply from its code, sequential coding is not a very effective system and is usually only seen in organisations where there are very few stock parts.

Significant coding

1.6 Many organisations use a **significant coding system** whereby each digit or sequence of digits signifies a particular quality of the item. Another approach is to design a code where each character or digit conveys meaning. Significant codes are longer than sequential ones as redundancy needs to be built in so that items not yet coded can be added later.

1.7 Where practical, codes should not be so long that they cannot be recalled. For example if a 12-digit code is being used, individual codes can be broken down into, for example, four lots of three numbers. Each lot may in turn refer to:

- The main group (electrical equipment)
- The subgroup (televisions)
- The manufacturer or supplier (Sony)
- The item number (Model 123)

1.8   Here is an example, taken from a manufacturer of machinery with three categories of assembly items. Each part has a six-digit part number.

First digit	*Second digit*	*Third–sixth digits*
1 major component	1 machine shop	Four-figure bin number
2 minor component	2 paint shop	
3 consumable	3 assembly	
4 quality control		

2	3	4091

So part number 234091 is a minor component required by the assembly department to be found in bin number 4091.

1.9   A system of significant coding can be very helpful in cases where there is a large number of parts which are used in a variety of locations, and the code 'signifies' features of the product such as, in the example above, its use, its nature and its location.

Letter codes

1.10   Letter codes offer 24 symbols ('I' and 'O' are customarily not used). As the letters can form words they can be easy to remember. In use the system can have certain drawbacks, with sequences that do not make words proving difficult to remember and possible confusion when one letter refers to more than one product. Letter codes can be effective however with a small product range or when linked to a numeric or symbolic code.

1.11   A variation on the two themes above is the **alphanumeric code**. This is a combination of numeric codes and letter codes and may give the advantages of both systems. There is no 'ruling' as to the amount of letters and numbers used and the code could be letters first or numbers first. An example might be TKM 5834 where the letters might represent the supplier or the product ('TKM' here is taken from Thyssen Krupp Materials but bears no relationship to any actual code).

Colour-based coding

1.12   Colour codes have limitations as most coding systems are now linked to IT-based stock control systems where colour is not recognised. However, colour can be appropriate, particularly when linked to hazardous goods or for distinguishing between contents held in drums, pipelines, cylinders etc. Even so, it is limited in use for stock management.

1.13   **Colour marking** is a variation on this theme. Here, code numbers are sometimes supplemented by colour marking on the materials or parts themselves. This can be done with metals, cables, small component parts, drums of oil and various other stores. If the colours are not too complicated, this system provides a ready means of identification by sight. In the case of small electrical components, for instance, it may be that although there is no satisfactory means of stamping a code number on the item, it is quite satisfactory to use colours instead. For metals, a colour code could be as follows.

- Green for iron
- Blue for steel
- Black for aluminium
- Red for copper
- White for zinc

1.14   Secondary colours can then be used to give more information, eg blue and red to indicate high-speed steel; blue, red and green to identify 18% tungsten high-speed steel, and so on.

Barcoding

1.15   This is an IT-based system whereby numerical codes are printed on or attached to stock items. This is done in the form of 'bars' which are a series of (usually) black stripes of varying thickness. If you are not familiar with warehouses and stock items, remember that most retail items have barcodes. This is certainly true of everything that is sold in supermarkets and also applies to books.

1.16   Barcodes are cheap to print and the reading technologies are varied and reliable. However the barcode is over 30 years old and, although it is effective for product recording and recognition, technology has moved on around it. Wireless techniques for transmitting barcode data across uncabled distances are potentially valuable for online inventory operations and are in extensive use by both centralised and hand-held recognition units.

1.17   Barcoding can serve many functions in warehousing.

- Verification of stock levels
- Identification of stock location
- Tracking and tracing the movement of goods and despatch details

1.18   Barcodes allow information relating to the various stock items to be transmitted quickly to all interested parties. This can apply to any part of the supply chain. The system that is most commonly used internationally is the European Article Numbering (EAN) system. Every organisation that is a member of EAN is allocated a unique block of numbers, the basic number containing 13 digits. The EAN format is as follows: 50 (the country code – in this case the UK) MMMMMXXXXXC. Here, MMMMM is the organisation prefix number, XXXXX is the item code and C is the final check digit. This description is somewhat simplified, but is sufficient for exam purposes.

1.19   We have just mentioned check digits. It is worth noting that a common problem associated with coding systems is that of inputting errors. This can be avoided by putting a 'check digit' into the code. This is a number calculated from the other numbers in the code. If someone attempts to input an incorrect code, the computer will reject it because the check digit will not tally with the other digits. This is known as a **self-validating code**.

Symbolic coding

1.20   A symbolic coding system uses symbols to represent an item or product. Symbolic coding is limited in use as it can be difficult to ensure that the symbol(s) will be recognised by anyone using the code. A relevant example relates to the handling of goods, with accepted international symbols for 'fragile', 'use no hooks', 'this way up' etc. Although this type of coding is essential in the warehouse environment it has no application in stock control and records.

Coding by the nature of the item

1.21   This involves the consideration of all stocked items by reference to their own inherent characteristics. The first stage is to collect similar items into a series of main groups such as raw materials, bought-out parts, tools, machinery spares, etc. Each of these groups is then subdivided into sub-groups or sections as far as the circumstances require. It must be understood that the groupings employed in any particular organisation will be arranged to suit that organisation.

Coding by the end use

1.22 This means arranging the code to correspond with the purposes for which the various items are eventually employed. For example, in a car factory the first division of materials would be into production stores and non-production stores, therefore the first coding subdivisions might be **PS** or **NP**. From there the products could be classified into engine components, body components, chassis, interior, electrical, etc. The next subdivision could be into the particular vehicle being made.

Technical spares

1.23 Where spares for vehicles, machines or equipment are stocked, the range can be very extensive and it will be found that the suppliers of these parts have usually already coded them by their own methods. In such circumstances, it is common practice to use the **maker's part numbers** as the last part of the stores code in the user's organisation.

Other bases of coding

1.24 Coding may also be arranged by any other method which seems desirable to suit special circumstances; for example, coding by reference to the location of items in the warehouse, to the source of supply, or to the customer who will eventually purchase the finished product or service.

Benefits and drawbacks of significant coding systems

1.25 Significant coding systems (of whatever type) are regarded as superior to sequential coding systems for a number of reasons.

- They allow the user to recognise, in broad or specific terms, the nature, feature and/or stores location of coded items
- They do not require a separate catalogue or index of codes, so usage is more efficient and less time-consuming
- They support standardisation and variety reduction, by clearly identifying differences or duplications in items within defined categories
- They allow flexibility for the addition and subtraction of items
- They facilitate staff training, by adding meaning to the coding system
- They facilitate complex and versatile computerised data processing, because of the inclusion of a range of relevant information.

1.26 The disadvantages of significant coding systems, if any, include the following.

- The costs of initial design, installation, implementation and staff training
- The need for agreement and integration with customer, supplier and internal stakeholder systems
- Reliance on IT systems, which are subject to risks of teething trouble, breakdown, security breach, data corruption, obsolescence and incompatibility.

2 Characteristics of a good coding system

Product codes vs product names

2.1 Stock records are difficult to maintain using a name-based system. As soon as quantities held reach a significant number it becomes essential to devise a system that categorises product types and allows for development of recognition codes. The development of a coding system brings a range of cross-company benefits other than just stock control.

2.2 All the techniques for tracing stock movements would be assisted by an efficient coding system. Coding has been defined by CIPS as:

'... a system of symbols, letters and/or numbers for the identification of items and components whereby each is given a complete and unique identification reference which cannot be confused with another and [which] can be recorded, retrieved and recognised throughout the enterprise and also by its customers where appropriate.'

2.3 It is not possible to use the full name of a product to describe it for the following reasons.

- Names can be easily confused. A major problem here is that different people often use a different name for the same thing. This means that, in a warehouse, it would be quite possible that staff member B would not be able to find something that had been named by staff member A because each individual uses a different name for the same item.
- Names do not provide any way of accurately categorising goods.
- Names are not easily input in computer systems.

2.4 Coding removes ambiguity. A correctly designed coding system eliminates any risk of confusion which might arise from a verbal description of a stock item. As a code is usually briefer than a description, there are savings in:

- time required for completing documentation
- time required for incorporating into a computerised stock control system
- data-storage capacity required in a computer system.

2.5 Industry norms such as sizing, standards and measures can help but these do have limitations when controlling ever-increasing quantities of stock. When dealing with stock it is necessary to have some logical basis for identification that is more precise and less involved.

Benefits of a good coding system

2.6 Jessop and Morrison detail the following principal advantages of a good coding system.

- It avoids repeated use of long descriptive titles.
- It accurately identifies all items.
- It prevents duplication of items.
- It assists standardisation and variety reduction.
- It provides a foundation for an efficient purchasing organisation.
- It forms a convenient basis for sorting and recording of documents.
- It simplifies recording.
- It is convenient for central analysis of unit storehouse records.
- It can be employed as a basis for stock control accounts.
- It may be used as a warehouse location system.

2.7 Key considerations when deciding on a coding system are the main purposes being served and the impact on other organisational functions. There will often be a conflict between operational and management requirements, and it is essential that the method implemented provides the optimum benefit to the company.

2.8 Quayle and Jones (in *Logistics – An Integrated Approach*) examine the main purposes of a coding system and the principal organisational functions that may be interested in its development. Their conclusions are as follows.

- Coding leads to better identification of physical materials in the factory or warehouse. This is of greatest interest to the stores, inspection and production functions.
- Coding provides easier reference for recording and analysis. This is of concern to the administrative and clerical functions.
- Coding offers a better means of identifying and classifying for charging value to jobs. This is the concern of the finance function.
- Coding is an aid to all activities of materials management and control. This is of significant importance to senior management.
- Coding is an aid to, or in many cases a prerequisite of, stock control systems.

Developing an effective coding system

2.9 When an organisation has considered and evaluated the main objectives that the coding system is required to achieve, consideration should be given to the main principles to follow in the development of an effective coding system.

- It must be capable of covering all items likely to be used, not only now but also in the future.
- It must be designed to suit the needs of the organisation.
- It must allow for expansion without duplication occurring.
- Each item must appear only once and the system must be designed to ensure this occurs.
- There must be a constant number of symbols or digits in all code references.
- Each group of symbols and/or digits must signify only one object.
- Descriptions and specifications on which the system is based should be as brief as possible while maintaining accuracy.

Requirements of an effective coding system

2.10 There are a number of requirements for an effective coding system.

- Each code should be unique and certain. Each item should have only one possible code number that can be easily identified from the structure of the code.
- It should not be possible for two people to allocate a different code number to a single stock item.
- The coding system should be comprehensive and flexible, ie it should be possible to identify a code number for every item.
- The coding system should be capable of expanding to accommodate new items.
- The code should be as brief as possible, having regard to the amount of detail needed in any analysis of items that may need to be performed.
- The coding system should be centrally controlled. It should not be possible for individuals independently to delete codes or add new codes to an existing system.

2.11 The elements of a successful coding system can be remembered using the mnemonic SUCCESS. The elements indicated by this acronym are, in many respects, a development of the above requirements and are as follows.

- **S**imple: the system should be easy enough for everyone to understand.
- **U**nique: each item should have only one code and each code should refer to a single item.
- **C**omprehensive: the system should cover all of the stock items.
- **C**onsistent: the same format should be used for all stock items.
- **E**xpandable: the format should allow for the expansion of the product range.
- **S**ignificant: all of the elements of the code should have some meaning or significance that can be conveyed to the user.
- **S**elf-validating: ideally a check digit could be employed within the code to prevent errors of input.

2.12 The first five characteristics of the SUCCESS concept are essential elements of all coding systems. Significant and self-validating codes are *desirable* elements.

2.13 A coding system should be flexible and last a long time to derive proper benefits from it. It is not something which is changed every quarter or every other year. Therefore, the long-term requirements of materials for the organisation should be kept in mind while providing the digits or alphabets for the items. The coding system should not only have enough vacant spaces but should be flexible enough to suit the requirements of the long-term future.

2.14 The coding system should be precise and should ensure a unique code for reach item. A proper dictionary or vocabulary for the decoding should be made while installing a coding system. The number of letters or digits should be the same for all items.

2.15 The total number of letters or numbers should not be so large as to lose its immediate meaning to the user of the material. Seven to ten digits or spaces are adequate for many of the coding systems. However, with a high degree of computerisation it is likely that more digits would be used.

2.16 A good system of coding helps in the standardisation of items in the inventory. Standardisation means reducing the variety of items stocked in the inventory to a workable minimum, by fixing sizes, shapes, dimensions and other quality characteristics of the item. For instance, paint may be bought from a number of suppliers in different sizes of containers and different shades of colour. All of these might increase the inventory of paints considerably. It may be more efficient if the number of suppliers is cut down, if the variety in the sizes of the containers is reduced and if the number of shades of colours is also reduced.

2.17 Some organisations design their own coding system although many adopt one of the existing, widely known systems. These latter systems have the advantages of being interchangeable across organisational boundaries and throughout the supply chain. This means that it is possible for organisations to adopt coding systems devised by their competitors.

2.18 Here are some examples of widely used coding systems.

- NATO (North Atlantic Treaty Organisation): it developed a comprehensive coding system that, although designed for military purposes, is used by many non-military organisations.
- Shell Oil developed the MESC (Materials Equipment Standards and Code) system as well as the Pantone® colour system for the printing industry. Many companies in the same industry have adopted both of these systems.

- Various national and international bodies have developed systems. An example would be the Standard Industrial Classification (SIC) system developed by the UK Statistics Office.

3 Order tracking technologies

Barcoding

3.1 A barcode system is a network of hardware and software, consisting primarily of mobile computer, printers, handheld scanners and infrastructure, and supporting software. Barcode systems are used to automate data collection where hand recording is not timely or cost effective.

3.2 The hardware required for managing barcode stock are hand-held terminals and mobile and mid-range thermal transfer printers. The hand-held terminal software is used for receiving and despatching goods in the warehouse and doing stock counts. The data collected on the terminal is then uploaded to the PC either in batch mode or in real time to provide a perpetual inventory. The barcode printing module enables product and location barcodes to be printed on portable thermal transfer printers.

Inventory control and product tracking with barcodes

3.3 There are many different types of stock that need tracking and most warehouse management systems do it by using barcode labels or tags. In this context, products usually fall in to three categories.

- **Commodity products.** This type of product does not need tracking down to individual product units, but we need to know when it came in and how much of it we have with perpetual inventory control. An item with a specific product code can be held across many locations and the total quantity of the commodity in stock can be assessed easily with the 'stock by location' report and the 'stock by product' report. The movement of product as a result of sale, goods in or simply moving it to a new location is accompanied with a barcode scan providing an electronic record of the transaction.
- **Serial numbered products.** User products such as televisions that have individual serial numbers. When they are sold the individual serial number is removed from stock so that at any one point in time a complete list of serial numbers is held as well as the total number of units in stock.
- **Batch numbers.** The use of batch numbers is a combination of a serial number and a commodity product. The best example would be a pallet of bags of flour where it is necessary to track the data that the bags came in and their batch number without having to serially number each individual bag.

3.4 Barcode tracking is now a sophisticated operation using a mix of hardware and software to recognise product, locate product and facilitate the movement of product through to the wholesaler, retailer or customer.

3.5 Barcode software allows us to receive items into inventory quickly, easily and accurately. When the goods are received into stock a goods received note will be issued, quoting the purchase order number, usually with copies to the warehouse, the accounts department and the purchasing department. In many cases this could be an electronic document. If the goods were not barcoded when delivered most software packages will allow us to print our own labels.

The goods will be received using a handheld mobile computer with a barcode reader. This will scan barcodes and capture lot or serial number details to enter into inventory, verifying immediately that the correct product and quantities have been received.

3.6 Barcode software and hardware allows an up to date record of physical inventory to be kept. When linked to a warehouse or inventory management system stock numbers and location can be recorded. Stock checks and physical records can be checked by scanning the barcodes.

3.7 We will discuss RFID tagging shortly. One advantage that RFID technology holds over barcoding is that the scanning can be carried out at a distance. With barcodes, the barcode needs a clear line of sight to be scanned physically.

EPC coding

3.8 Coding underpins much of the movement of goods through to delivery to the final customer. The role of coding enables real-time inventory management and delivery tracking. The application of computer-based systems to effective stock control by means of barcodes and RFID technology has brought an arguably staid business area to the forefront of business awareness and customer service.

3.9 The Electronic Product Code (EPC) is the next generation of product identification from barcodes. Although barcodes have limitations (they require line-of-sight for scanning, have limited encoding capacity, and cannot receive and store information), they are currently used by more than 1 million organisations in more than 140 countries across more than 23 industries. They clearly remain important to supply chain operations.

3.10 The EPC is a set of identification coding or numbering standards. Unlike the barcodes commonly used to distinguish a can of soup from a box of chocolate chip biscuits, the EPC can identify a specific can of soup or box of biscuits by its unique ID number. The EPC contains no personal information. Some experts believe that in years to come the EPC – together with RFID – will be as common as the barcode is today.

3.11 It is projected that barcodes and EPCs will co-exist for many years to come. The EPC is a simple code that uniquely identifies objects such as items, cases, pallets, and locations, in the supply chain. The EPC is built around a basic hierarchical idea that can be used to express a wide variety of different, existing numbering systems.

3.12 Like many current numbering schemes used in commerce, the EPC is divided into numbers that identify the manufacturer and product type. But the EPC uses an extra set of digits, a serial number, to identify unique items. The EPC is the key to the information about the product it identifies that exists in the EPC global network.

3.13 An EPC number contains the following elements.

- Header – identifies the length, type, structure, version, and generation of EPC.
- Manager number – identifies the company or company entity.
- Object class – similar to a stock keeping unit (SKU).
- Serial number – the specific instance of the object class being tagged.

3.14 Additional fields may also be used as part of the EPC in order to properly encode and decode information from different numbering systems into their native, human-readable, forms. This enables users to exchange EPC-related data with trading partners through the EPC global network.

3.15 EPC is central to the long-term success of RFID technology. A key aspect of EPC is the application of serialisation to all product codes – the idea that every product has its own unique identifier. Underestimating the impact that serialisation will have on the supply chain could seriously damage supply chain partners' ability to compete effectively over the long term.

3.16 Designed to be stored on an RFID tag, the EPC is a unique number that identifies a specific item in a supply chain. Besides holding product information the EPC can carry such information as date of manufacture or point of origin and other information and data that can then be transmitted electronically.

Radio frequency identification (RFID)

3.17 RFID is a technology that uses devices attached to objects that transmit data to an RFID receiver. These devices can be large pieces of hardware the size of a small book, (like those attached to ocean containers) or very small devices inserted into a label on a package. RFID has advantages over barcodes: it can hold more data; it can change the stored data as processing occurs; it does not require line-of-sight to transfer data; and it is very effective in harsh environments where barcode labels won't work.

3.18 RFID is a physical technology (tags, readers, antennas, middleware), and is winning the day as the standard to be used in much of the retail landscape for holding and capturing the unique serial number of an item in the supply chain. However, the end is not the technology, but the value that can be gained from the data generated by implementing it.

3.19 Long checkout lines at the supermarket are one of the biggest complaints about the shopping experience. Soon, these lines could disappear when barcodes are replaced by smart labels, ie by RFID tags. RFID tags are intelligent barcodes that can talk to a networked system to track every product that you put in your shopping cart.

3.20 Imagine going to the supermarket, filling up your cart and walking right out of the door. No longer will you have to wait as someone rings up each item in your trolley one at a time. Instead, RFID tags will communicate with an electronic reader that will detect every item in the cart and ring up each almost instantly. The reader will be connected to a large network that will send information on your products to the retailer and product manufacturers. Your bank will then be notified and the amount of the bill will be deducted from your account.

3.21 RFID tags are now used to track product worldwide. Many manufacturers use the tags to track the location of each product they make from the time it is made until it is pulled off the shelf and put in a shopping trolley. Outside the realm of retail merchandise, RFID tags are tracking vehicles, airline passengers, Alzheimer's patients and pets. Some critics say RFID technology is becoming too much a part of our lives.

3.22 Almost everything that we buy from retailers has a barcode printed on it. This helps manufacturers and retailers keep track of inventory. Barcodes also give valuable information about the quantity of products being bought and, to some extent, the consumers buying them. These codes serve as product identifiers made of machine-readable parallel bars that store binary code.

3.23 Going through the checkout line involves the same process of scanning each barcode on each item. A barcode is a read-only technology, meaning that it cannot send out any information.

3.24 RFID tags are an improvement over barcodes because the tags have read and write capabilities. Data stored on RFID tags can be changed, updated and locked. Some stores that have begun using RFID tags have found that the technology offers a better way to track merchandise for stocking and marketing purposes. Through RFID tags, stores can see how quickly the products leave the shelves and which shoppers are buying them.

3.25 RFID tags will not entirely replace barcodes in the near future – far too many retail outlets currently use barcode scanners in billions of transactions every year. However, as time goes on we will definitely see more products tagged with RFIDs and an increased focus on wireless transactions.

Warehouse management using RFID

3.26 In order to improve productivity and control, warehouses are seriously considering the use of RFID tags for day-to-day operations. This wireless technology increases efficiency of warehouse management because, unlike barcodes which must be scanned manually to feed in the information on the computers, RFID tags broadcast a signal with information about the product they are attached to and about the location of the product in the warehouse. RFID technology provides a method to aid data collection and product identification in the supply chain management and warehouse operation.

3.27 One of the main purposes of using RFID is to increase warehouse efficiency by reducing labour and logistic costs. It is cost-efficient because the warehouses can now streamline several operational areas inside their premises. For example, picture a typical warehouse where staff receive boxes of stock accompanied by paperwork detailing items in the delivery. Staff members then manually check each box's contents against the manifest.

3.28 The drawback of this method is that store staff cannot see what items are in which box, or whether items are missing until each box has been individually checked. Many of these operation areas might benefit from radio frequency technology. This wireless technology in warehouses can help establish a simple paperless, online communication between operations and the staff member's computer.

3.29 RFID-based warehouse management brings several benefits that can eliminate current drawbacks with the help of advanced scanning. Capabilities include the following.

- Improved efficiency by using RFID tags that facilitate automatic data entry rather than manually making entries of stock first on paper and then into computer terminals. This eliminates the time required for data entry, sending paper orders to the warehouse and filling and maintaining the paperwork.
- Wireless warehouse technology that can provide timely information and integration of warehouse data into the ERP system.
- RFID ensures timely and accurate information for invoicing, purchase order payments and inventory tracking.
- It reduces inventory errors, ensuring that the inventory reported is indeed available. By tracking pieces more exactly, companies can more accurately detail what has sold in the last business day, and improve the accuracy of their forecasts about what inventory is actually needed.
- It can strengthen security against product theft, loss and counterfeiting. RFID reduces inventory errors, ensuring that the inventory reported is indeed available. By tracking pieces

more exactly, companies can more accurately detail what has sold in the last business day, and improve the accuracy of their forecasts about what inventory is actually needed.

- It helps in reducing errors in order fulfilment and shipping, not only lowering the monetary cost of errors, but also keeping customer satisfaction and return business levels high.

Delivery to the customer

3.30 Location tracking is not one single technology. Rather, it is the convergence of several technologies that can be merged to create systems that track inventory, livestock or vehicle fleets. Similar systems can be created to deliver location-based services to wireless devices.

3.31 In distribution and logistics delivering many types of products, **track and trace** refers to a process of determining the current and past locations (and other information) of a unique item or property. This concept can be supported by means of reckoning and reporting of the position of vehicles and containers with the property of concern, stored, for example, in a real-time database.

3.32 Another approach is to report the arrival or departure of the object, recording the identification of the object, the location where observed, the time, and the status. This approach leaves the task to verify the reports regarding consistency and completeness. An example of this method might be the package tracking provided by shippers, such as FedEx or UPS.

3.33 Track and trace technology is in common use. It enables delivery companies and their customers to track product deliveries through a combination of IT systems and GPS (Global Positioning Systems) as found in cars or mobile phones. The systems allow customers to order delivery to home or work and check the progress of the delivery *en route*.

7

Chapter summary

- An effective coding system is essential for the management of large inventories.
- Types of coding system include numeric, significant, letter codes, colour-based coding, barcoding, symbolic coding etc.
- Use of product codes is more efficient and less prone to ambiguity than use of product names.
- Elements of a successful coding system are captured by the mnemonic SUCCESS: simple, unique, comprehensive, consistent, expandable, significant and self-validating.
- Barcoding and EPC coding are important techniques in product tracking.
- RFID is a newer technology that has significant advantages compared with barcoding.

Self-test questions

Numbers in brackets refer to the paragraphs above where your answers can be checked.

1   What are the main advantages of an effective coding system? (Figure 7.1)

2   Explain how a significant coding system works.(1.6–1.9)

3   List some of the functions of barcoding in warehouse management. (1.17)

4   List benefits of significant coding systems as compared with other coding systems. (1.25)

5   List the advantages of a coding system as identified by Jessop and Morrison. (2.6)

6   What are the main requirements of a good coding system? (2.10)

7   List three categories of stock that need to be tracked by technologies such as barcoding. (3.3)

8   What are the four elements of an EPC code? (3.13)

9   What are the advantages of RFID tags compared with barcodes? (3.17)

10 List some of the functions of RFID technology in warehouse management. (3.29)

CHAPTER 8

Warehousing Equipment

Assessment criteria and indicative content

2.2 Describe the use of product coding in inventory operations

- The use of RFID technologies

2.3 Describe the use of warehousing equipment

- Materials handling equipment
- Palletisation and unit loads
- Packing and packaging
- Environmental standards for packaging
- The use of automation in warehousing

Section headings

1 Storage equipment and systems
2 Materials handling equipment and systems
3 Principles of packaging
4 Automation in warehousing

1 Storage equipment and systems

Palletisation and unit loads

1.1 The efficiency of warehouse operations depends crucially on the systems in place for storage and materials handling. We begin by looking at the choice of storage equipment and systems. There are several main principles we need to consider.

- The characteristics of goods and unit loads we hold
- The effective use of the cube verses stock accessibility
- Increased productivity (speed of throughput etc)
- Integration with current IT systems
- Stock accountability and tracking
- Personnel health and safety
- Overall system cost and speed of integration

1.2 By considering all of these principles we will be able to arrive at a selection of storage equipment that is suitable for our specific needs. We do not necessarily have to have our storage equipment custom-built, but we need to understand all the issues so that we can obtain equipment that provides the most economic use of space at the lowest cost.

1.3 Firstly, a word about **unitisation**, which is the use of unit loads. A unit load is a number of similar items or packages assembled into one batch. They are usually cube-shaped and are capable of being stacked (usually in some kind of racking or shelving). Examples of unit loads might be pallets or containers such as cage pallets or post pallets (see later in this chapter) or tote bins. Unit loads are capable of being handled by a variety of handling equipment. Pallets are of a standard size and are subject to an ISO standard.

1.4 The use of standard unit loads allows the movement of loads between organisations using different materials handling equipment. Unitisation provides a number of advantages.

- It reduces the number of journeys required
- Space can be used more efficiently
- It enables the use of storage and handling equipment because the same equipment can be used to move and store different items
- It might reduce losses arising from damage and pilferage

Storage without racking

1.5 It is possible to store goods in a warehouse without using any racking. The two methods of doing this are block stacking and the use of post pallets and cage pallets.

1.6 **Block stacking**. Many items can be stacked on top of each other. This may be because of their own in-built strength or because they are packed in cases or cartons that can withstand a given amount of weight. Where this is possible it would be wasteful to store the goods on, say, pallet racking as this would take up more space and cost more money. See Figure 8.1.

Figure 8.1 *Block stacking*

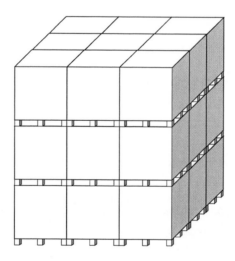

1.7 The great advantage of block stacking is that the use of the cube can approach 100%, whereas with pallet racking the maximum might be only 50%. However, block stacking is not suitable for every operation – even when the goods can be block stacked. This is because of the way in which the stack works.

1.8 From Figure 8.1 we can see that the goods at the top of each column must have been received after the goods at the bottom of the column. If we are required to send goods out in strict first in, first out order we are going to be faced with a problem. Every time we send goods out we will have to take the stack to pieces to get at the oldest stock. The same would apply if the goods had to be issued by serial number – we would spend too much time trying to find an individual item.

1.9 **Post pallets and cage pallets**. Some goods are sufficiently strong to withstand the weight of other goods above them but their shape means that block stacking would be dangerous because the stack would be unstable. Other goods may be incapable of being block stacked because they would be crushed.

1.10 We can get around these two problems by using post pallets or cage pallets. These pallets work because the weight is taken not by the goods but by the pallet itself. They consist of a pallet with an upright column at each corner. The feet of the pallet above fit over the column of the pallet below. They are mostly made of steel and so can be stacked to a great height. Post pallets are usually used for regularly shaped goods and cage pallets for irregularly shaped goods, which are likely to be unstable. These two variants are illustrated in Figure 8.2.

Figure 8.2 *Post pallets and cage pallets*

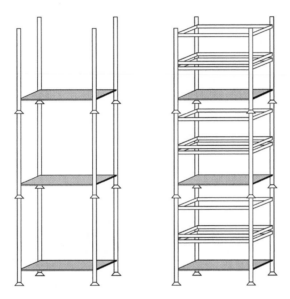

Types of racking

1.11 Warehouses will usually require some racking and this should be as flexible as possible to suit changing requirements. Most pallet racking and shelving is adjustable and other types of racking achieve their flexibility by offering a wide range of different sized locations as part of their design – plastic bins are an example. If we have a variety of location sizes we will save space as we can store small goods in small locations and large goods in large locations.

1.12 There are many types of racking available. One of the most common is **pallet racking**. Most pallets are made of wood, although they can be made of steel, aluminium and plastic. There are two basic types: the two-way entry (where the pallet can be picked up from the front or the back), and the four-way entry (where the pallet can be picked up from any side). The two types are illustrated in Figure 8.3.

Figure 8.3 *Two types of pallet*

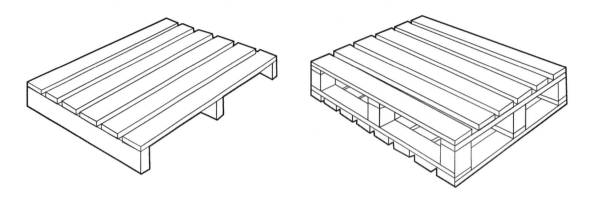

1.13 Pallet racking must be able to support the pallet and still allow access for the materials handling equipment (usually a forklift truck or stacker or pallet truck) that is used to load and unload the pallets. To achieve this, the racking consists of beams that are supported by end frames bolted to the floor.

1.14 The position of the beams can be adjusted upwards or downwards so that we can vary the size of the locations. Although pallet racking is adjustable, this facility is, in practice, not used very often. It is illustrated in Figure 8.4 (using four-way entry pallets).

Figure 8.4 *Adjustable pallet racking*

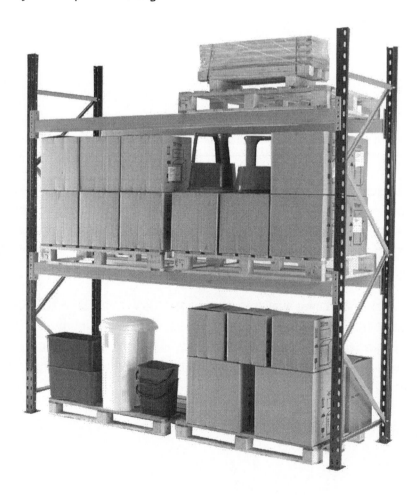

1.15 If we need more space in the warehouse, perhaps owing to growth of the business, we may be forced to increase capacity by adding more racking. This can only be done by reducing the width of our aisles. Ordinary ('counterbalanced') forklift trucks need fairly wide aisles to get access to the racks. However, if we reduce the width of the aisles we will need to use a different sort of truck called a **reach truck**. These can have the same lifting capacity as a counterbalanced truck but require less aisle space.

1.16 Some are fitted with telescopic units so that they can reach higher than forklift trucks. These allow the use of high-density racking – racking which uses the full height of the building and allows full use of the 'cube'. A variation on this theme is **very narrow aisle** racking. This uses even narrower aisles than those used in conjunction with reach trucks. The system usually utilises an 'order picker' which travels up and down the aisle on rails. It would have a cab, which would move vertically and would be where the operator is. The forks operate by means of a swivelling 'turret' which allows them to access pallets on both sides of the aisle.

1.17 **Shelving** is probably the most common type of storage medium. Most shelving is adjustable in terms of the height between the shelves. Most industrial shelving consists of an enclosed frame into which the shelves are fitted as required. Figure 8.5 illustrates adjustable shelving. Although most shelving is used for manual picking we can pick from it mechanically by using an order picker, as described above.

Figure 8.5 *Adjustable shelving*

1.18 **Small parts storage**. Many warehouses have a need to store small objects. These may be parts for machinery or any other items that do not need to be kept separate from each other in some form of packaging. There are two problems with objects such as these: their size means they can be easily lost; and the quantity we need to hold can vary across time. These two problems can be overcome by using plastic storage bins.

1.19   These bins come either in the form of drawers in a cabinet or as separate bins that we can hang on a louvered panel. Both have two attributes that make them ideal for this type of storage.

- The bins themselves are moulded, which means that they won't allow small parts to escape. The alternative to plastic bins are bins made of steel.
- Many plastic bins, particularly the drawer types, can be divided up into smaller locations by using plastic inserts. Where this is not possible, as with many designed to be used with louvered panels, the bins themselves may come in a dozen or more shapes and sizes.

1.20   Figure 8.6 gives a representation of this type of storage.

Figure 8.6 *Moulded plastic bins*

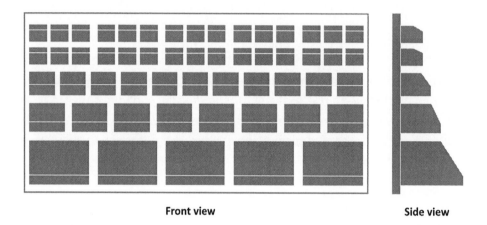

Front view   **Side view**

1.21   **Cantilever racking** (or antler racking as it is sometimes called: see Figure 8.7) is designed to hold long goods. The system consists of a row of pillars from which a number of arms protrude. The goods are stored by resting them on the arms of two or more pillars. This type of racking is useful for storing things such as timber, particularly in larger sizes that don't need to be supported along their whole length, pipes made of steel or plastic, metal bars of all sizes, or ladders.

Figure 8.7 *Cantilever racking*

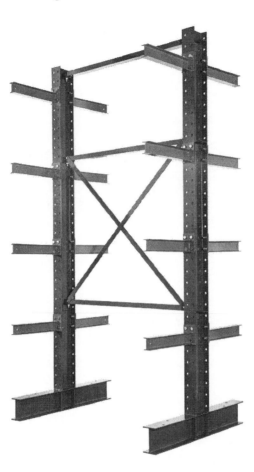

1.22 The problem with cantilever racking is that its storage density can be very low. This is because of the need to pick the goods mechanically owing to their weight, which means that the aisles between the racks have to be quite wide. Also the racking itself has to have a wide base to stand on because it cannot be built back-to-back like pallet racking and shelving.

1.23 **Live storage** is where the goods are allowed to move within the rack, usually on rollers under the power of gravity. A typical installation consists of a rack in which the load supports, which are usually beams or shelves, have been replaced with rollers set at an angle sloping down towards the front of the rack. Because there are rollers involved, this sort of installation is only suitable for goods that are packed in a container that can be placed on the rollers without any chance of becoming jammed or spilling the contents. This means that palletised goods and goods that come in small cartons, such as household electrical equipment, are ideal for this type of installation.

1.24 Any goods placed in a live storage installation will move forward down the slope until they reach a stop at the front of the rack. When the first item is removed from the front of a run the remaining items will again move downwards. Thus the next to be picked is always presented to the picker at the front of each run. An example is shown in Figure 8.8.

Figure 8.8 *Live storage*

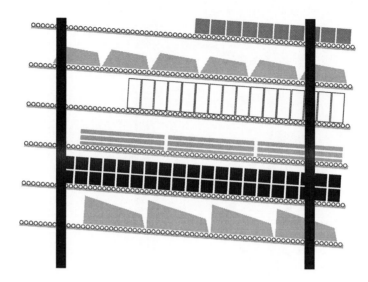

1.25 One of the advantages of this system is that the goods are always presented to the picker in the same order in which they were loaded into the back of the rack. In other words this system will ensure we adhere strictly to a policy of FIFO. Because of the strict way it applies FIFO, systems like these are often used for foodstuffs.

1.26 Another advantage of this sort of racking is that, because the goods are presented to us, we don't have to move very far to pick them. With some items in cartons we may be able to present as many as 80 different products to our picker in a picking face measuring just 2m x 2m.

1.27 In a **mobile racking** installation the racking is mounted on rails and it moves up and down the warehouse floor. This can be done with any sort of racking – pallets, shelves, small parts etc. The great advantage is that the number of warehouse aisles is reduced to just one and access is gained to each of the racks by opening the aisle at the appropriate place. This can save space to a very high degree. Most mobile racking in warehouses is electrically powered but much smaller manual versions are sometimes used for document storage or storage of small parts.

1.28 The main disadvantage with mobile racking is that it can be very slow to operate and use. There is a good reason for this: each rack may weigh several hundred tons when loaded and we may need to move several racks to gain access to the one we want. Even in smaller installations where we may be able to move several racks at a time there is always a delay while we open the correct aisle. The mobile racking principle is illustrated in Figure 8.9.

Figure 8.9 *Mobile racking*

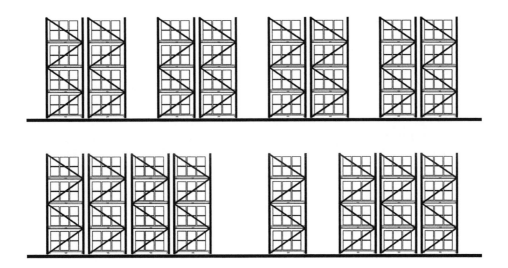

1.29 **Drive-in and drive-through racking**. These are pallet-based racking systems that allow access for forklift trucks. If access is from one end only the racking is referred to as 'drive-in'. If pallets are fed in at one end and removed at the other (support is vertical rather than horizontal, apart from maintaining structural integrity) then the term 'drive-through' is used.

1.30 Drive-in racks are designed for storing large quantities of similar pallets. These are stored depth-wise, behind each other, on continuous pallet-supporting rails. As a result, a high storage density is obtained ensuring a high utilisation of floor space. These racks are often used where space is expensive (eg in coldstores).

Efficient utilisation of warehouse space

1.31 We have considered the need to maximise the use of space and flow of items in the warehouse at some length but there are a few other aspects of this and ways to achieve it that we need to consider.

1.32 **Good housekeeping**: this contributes to the efficiency of the warehouse. Aisles should be kept clear of obstacles and rubbish and items should be put away in their correct locations as soon as possible after they have been received into the warehouse. It is also important to ensure that items are picked quickly and efficiently when they are required.

1.33 **Traffic flow**: as we have already seen, there should be a flow system in the warehouse that goes some way towards ensuring that there is no congestion of stock pickers. This is one of the main benefits of the 'throughflow' or 'U shaped' systems discussed in an earlier chapter.

1.34 **Stock picking** is the process of removing items from the storage racks and spaces so that they can be issued to user departments or despatched to customers. Lists of requirements (picking lists) are often used so that personnel can 'pick' the items on the list. There are two variations on this theme: sectional picking and travelling picking.

1.35 **Sectional picking** (or zoned picking): stock items are separated by classification (eg component parts; lubricants etc). Personnel will collect them from the storage area and take them to a marshalling area where the whole consignment is consolidated ('kit marshalled') for despatch.

1.36 **Travelling picking**: personnel make journeys around the warehouse to collect all of the items on the list until all the items for one shipment have been collected. IT can assist by printing off a suitable list and two recent developments of this are:

- A kind of 'SatNav' on the forklift truck to guide the driver so that items are picked in a logical order
- The driver wears headphones through which the computer tells him in which order to pick the items so that, again, this is done in a logical order.

1.37 **Security**: the main threats here are from internal pilferage (many warehouses store 'attractive' items) and external theft. Measures designed to protect warehouses against both were listed in an earlier chapter.

1.38 **Long-term flexibility**: the types of items and/or their volume might change over time and any planning of warehouse layout needs to take these into account so that changes can be carried out efficiently.

2 Materials handling equipment and systems

Manual handling

2.1 As we have seen, items arriving at the warehouse have to be unloaded from their transport, put away for storage, and eventually picked and despatched to internal or external customers. These activities all involve the need for materials handling solutions.

2.2 A first option is **manual handling**. This can be useful where loads are light and the distances to be travelled are small. However, this will not be a suitable solution when goods are heavy or large in volume and/or need to be moved frequently. Also, warehouses are often subject to regulations which require employers to ensure that employees' health and safety is not jeopardised by lifting and carrying. Where manual handling is not appropriate, there are other possible solutions.

2.3 **Trolleys** can be used to move goods. At their simplest, these might be similar to supermarket trolleys. There is also the platform truck (sometimes known as a 'pallet truck') that can move heavier loads. These are not powered but use hydraulic systems to raise pallets from the floor to allow the truck to be moved. The trucks can be steered by means of a steering handle. A variant on this theme is the tow-truck. This is similar to a pallet truck, but without the steering handle, and can be towed by a powered vehicle or tractor. Figure 8.10 shows a platform truck (in this case loaded with a cage pallet).

Figure 8.10 *A platform truck (or pallet truck)*

Powered materials handling equipment

2.4 Manual pallet trucks can only be used for moving moderate volumes although distances involved will probably not be great. To move large weights and volumes over longer distances, there is a battery powered version of the pallet truck (see Figure 8.11). As with any battery-operated truck the battery must be charged overnight although some organisations buy or lease such trucks with two battery packs so that one can be charged while the other is in use.

Figure 8.11 *A battery operated pallet truck*

8

2.5 Another variation on this theme is the battery-operated pallet truck that allows the operative to ride on it and steer it (Figure 8.12).

Figure 8.12 *A ride-on pallet truck*

2.6 Probably the most common and important form of materials handling device is the forklift truck. This is sometimes known as a 'counterbalanced truck' because its load, which is carried at the front, is counterbalanced by a cast iron weight at the rear. This 'counterbalancing' is particularly important when the truck is lifting loads up to high racking.

2.7 The range of forklifts is very wide with a spread from pedestrian-operated through to those able to handle 40-foot containers. The most common type used in warehouse operations are driver-operated counterbalanced forklift trucks. These are usually powered by diesel, liquid petroleum gas (LPG) or electricity (battery). The weight of the unloaded forklift is towards the rear of the vehicle, so that the load to be handled is counterbalanced over the vehicle's fulcrum (usually the front wheels).

2.8 Forklifts are suitable for carrying standard or unit loads. They are very manoeuverable, and are designed to suit the warehouse environment. They can stack to the required height, with a range of attachments to increase their height and depth reach if required.

2.9 Forklift trucks that operate inside warehouses should be battery powered because the fumes from diesel trucks are not a good idea indoors and extraction plants are extremely expensive. Diesel trucks, which often have greater carrying capacity than battery powered ones, are often used in stockyards and/or for loading and unloading lorries in the open air. A battery-operated forklift truck is shown in Figure 8.13.

Figure 8.13 *A battery powered forklift truck*

Advantages and disadvantages of forklift trucks

2.10 The advantages and disadvantages of forklift trucks are summarised in Table 8.1.

Table 8.1 *Forklift trucks*

ADVANTAGES	DISADVANTAGES
Wide range of types available	Costs of purchase, lease, maintenance etc.
Can be gas or electrically powered, for sustainable use	Costs of staff training (driver accreditation required)
Suitability for carrying standard or unit loads	May be less suitable for non-standard, heavy loads and very high stacking
Can stack to the required height, enabling use of cubic capacity	Require wide aisles and turning areas (compared to narrow-aisle trucks and reach trucks
Can carry large loads (depending on size of truck)	Battery-powered trucks may create recharge space and down-time issues
Versatility: attachments can be added to increase the range of materials handled	Health and safety risks (as with any form of mobile heavy equipment)

2.11 Another means of moving items in a warehouse is a **conveyor**. These can take the form of belts, rollers, pulleys, wheels and chains and can be powered mechanically or electrically. Also, gravity inclines can be used to move items from an upper floor to a lower one. Conveyors are useful for moving large goods over short distances.

2.12 Some warehouses might use a variation on the conveyor theme which is the **monorail**. These are single overhead rails to which hooks or small trolleys can be fitted.

2.13 Some warehouses are **fully automated**. Such systems are very expensive to install but might be useful where there is a high turnover of goods in a large area and a large number of repetitive activities. Clearly, before any such system is installed a full investment appraisal would be required to ensure that it would pay for itself over time.

2.14 In an automated system, traditional types of materials handling equipment are replaced by **automated guided vehicles** (AGVs). These move the items around the warehouse. They may be combined with computer-controlled robotic equivalents of forklift trucks so that one member of staff can put items away and pick them simply by entering codes into a computer.

2.15 All materials handling equipment represents a major investment for an organisation even if it is leased rather than purchased (which is a very popular option). Because of this the equipment should be stored safely and securely when not in use and care and maintenance requirements should be documented in the operating procedures. Personnel responsible for operating materials handling equipment should be trained in its care and use and the equipment should be regularly serviced in line with the manufacturer's recommendations. Lease agreements will often include such servicing.

2.16 The following key considerations or principles should be used when selecting and defining the use of handling systems and equipment.

- Elimination of unnecessary movement and minimisation of necessary movement
- Selection of the most appropriate handling methods to meet requirements
- Provision of adequate handling capacity
- Integration of handling with other operations
- Thorough and effective operator training
- Effective equipment maintenance
- Overall control of position and movement

3 Principles of packaging

Definitions of packaging

3.1 Your syllabus refers to both packing and packaging, but it is not clear what distinction (if any) is intended here. In this section we use the term 'packaging'.

3.2 The following are two definitions of packaging.

- 'The art, science and technology of preparing goods for transport and sale'
- 'A means of ensuring the safe delivery of a product to the consumer in sound condition and at minimum cost' (British Standards Institution).

Functions of packaging

3.3 Packaging fulfils the following functions.

- To protect and preserve a product or the environment from physical, chemical and mechanical damage, deterioration or contamination
- To facilitate ease of handling
- To communicate information, for example, safety instructions
- To act as a marketing aid, through appearance and presentation

3.4 In addition to protecting products, packages should be easy to handle, convenient to store, readily identifiable, secure and of a shape that makes the best use of space. There are trade-offs between these factors that will affect the product and the materials handling process. For example, the packaging required to protect an awkwardly shaped item may have to be balanced against the optimum shape for handling or use of space.

3.5 Goods received into the warehouse from suppliers might be broken down into individual packets, which creates a need to dispose of the packaging material. Conversely, when we select these individual packages for despatch we will require packaging material to ensure the safe transportation of the goods to the customer. Considerable savings in both the receipts and despatch departments can be made if we introduce a process of internal recycling. Surplus packaging material should be collected for external recycling.

3.6 Certain hazardous materials require extensive packaging in storage and transit and legal regulations often require that the movement of dangerous goods must be supervised by a qualified person, a dangerous goods safety advisor (DGSA).

3.7 Most goods will deteriorate to some degree whilst in storage and stock will need to be protected against premature deterioration. Packaging can be used for this, which, apart from its primary function of protecting goods in transit, also assists preservation. Some areas of concern where good packaging can help could be as follows.

- Dust, water, and vapour-proofing
- Identification of hazards, including static electricity

3.8 Some goods may be delivered in bulk by suppliers and we will need to break this bulk down into smaller pack sizes. Some products may be sold as individual items and in these circumstances additional packaging may well be needed to protect the goods in both storage and transit.

3.9 Some goods also require packaging for cushioning against damage, which could include the use of Jiffy bags, bubble wrap or foam inside the external packaging. This is known as 'dunnage'. The common thread through all of this is that nearly all goods require some packaging. They also need to be clearly identified, including any associated hazardous labelling. Any such labelling must be clearly visible.

Environmental standards for packaging

3.10 Environmental management has become increasingly important over recent years as the volume of environmental legislation and regulations increases. All businesses, from offices and shops to businesses in sectors such as agriculture and chemicals, have legal environmental obligations that they must meet.

3.11 To ensure compliance an organisation should carry out a risk assessment as part of an overall review of environmental impact. Carrying out the risk assessment also gives the opportunity to identify ways to improve environmental performance generally, and to reduce energy costs and unnecessary waste.

3.12 Regulations in environmental standards aim to minimise the amount of waste packaging created and to ensure that packaging can be reused, recovered or recycled.

3.13 In organisations where packaging is a concern they may seek to adopt an internationally recognised standard such as those issued and audited by the British Standards Institution. Adopting a standard demonstrates to customers, in particular, that an organisation is serious about its obligations and about the impact of its environmental management. Many of the companies adopting a specific standard will also hold the environmental standard ISO 14001, again demonstrating their commitment to environmental issues.

3.14   An item is not considered to be packaging if it is part of a product and is necessary to preserve, contain or support the product during its lifespan and use (eg tea bags, and pots for house plants intended to stay with the plant throughout its life). The same is true of a disposable item designed to be used at the point of sale which does not fulfil a packaging function (eg drinks stirrers and plastic cutlery).

European standards

3.15   The European Union has given a high priority to environmental concerns regarding packaging. The turnover of the packaging industry in Western Europe represents around 2% of GDP. The food industry is the main user of packaging with nearly 60% of total packaging production. The range of packaging types and products is highly diversified and in many cases tailored to the needs of the users.

3.16   Packaging regulations within the European Union are developed by the European Committee for Standardisation (CEN). They issue Directives on packaging by publishing them in the *Official Journal of the European Union* (OJEU). Individual member countries of the European Union then adopt them into their legal systems. The depth of these regulations can be demonstrated by the recognition numbers and titles.

- EN 13432:2004: Requirements for packaging recoverable through composting and biodegradation
- EN 13427:2004: Requirements for the use of European Standards in the field of packaging and packaging waste
- EN 13428:2004: Requirements specific to manufacturing and composition.
- EN 13429:2004: Packaging reuse
- EN 13430:2004: Packaging requirements for packaging recoverable by material recycling
- EN 13431: 2004: Packaging requirements for packaging recoverable in the form of energy recovery, including the specification of minimum inferior calorific value.

International standards

3.17   Worldwide, many countries have their own concerns and issues regarding environmental packaging. For example, the USA and Australia have strict regulations relating to wooden cases in order to keep out unwanted agricultural pests. Other countries have laws relating to cardboard packaging and recyclablity. There has been a considerable amount of discussion in recent years with the objective of developing a common international understanding on packaging issues. Agreed standards are due to be published by the International Standards Organisation by the end of 2012.

3.18   The new ISO standards will be used by all companies involved in packaging including designers and manufacturers, recycling companies, retailers, branded goods manufacturers and manufacturers of packaging materials and inks. They will address the optimisation of packaging to minimise its environmental effect, the responsible use of heavy metals and other hazardous materials, the possible reuse of packages and the different modes of recycling.

3.19 This is said to mark the beginning of a new era in global manufacturing and distribution, where environmental aspects throughout the supply and recycle chain will already be considered in the packaging design process. The standards address the way the aspects of each package pertaining to the packaging system, reuse, material recycling, energy recovery and composting are related to each other before and after its use, and their optimisation as well.

3.20 The standards can be implemented by every responsible retailer, manufacturer and packaging supplier in their management system. Thereby they take responsibility for their specific part in the sustainable innovation of packages, packaged products, and recycling.

Packaging design requirements

3.21 It is advisable for both environmental and economic reasons to minimise the volume and weight of packaging used. The amount of packaging must be the minimum required to ensure the safety and hygiene of the packed product and to be acceptable to the consumer.

Packaging for recycling or reuse

3.22 Packaging that is intended to be recovered by recycling must be manufactured so that a percentage (by weight) of the material can be recycled. The percentage varies according to the type of material and the current standards in force.

3.23 Packaging intended to be recovered by energy recovery must be processed to allow for the maximum amount of energy to be recovered. This means that if any packaging waste is burned, it must produce more energy than is used by the incineration process.

3.24 Packaging should contain at least 50 per cent of combustible organic materials by weight. Combustible organic materials include paper, wood, cardboard and other organic fibres. Packaging intended for recovery by composting must be biodegradable so it doesn't slow down the composting process. To be biodegradable the packaging must decompose into carbon dioxide, biomass and water.

3.25 Reusable packaging must be capable of being used several times. Once at the end of its useful life, it must also meet the requirements for recycling, energy recovery or composting.

3.26 An organisation must ensure packaging does not contain high levels of noxious or hazardous substances and will have a minimum environmental impact when disposed of. The amount of heavy metals (cadmium, mercury, lead and hexavalent chromium, or any combination of these) must not exceed 100 parts per million by weight. These limits apply to packaging plus any packaging components, calculated as a whole unit. For example, components such as lids do not have to meet these limits independently.

Managing waste

3.27 The objective is to minimise packaging and only use packaging that meets environmental standards and that can be recovered or reused. Larger packaging producers will need to register with their environmental regulator and meet recycling and recovery targets.

3.28 It is essential to store and dispose of waste properly. Use a waste-disposal contractor who is authorised to treat and handle your kind of waste, and disposes of it at a site that has a permit for that kind of waste. There are extra controls on some special kinds of waste, such as hazardous waste, and on the storage of potentially harmful substances such as chemicals.

8

3.29   Manufacturers should aim to reduce packaging volume and weight in line with safety, hygiene and consumer acceptance, and to minimise the presence of hazardous substances in emissions when packaging waste is incinerated or landfilled. Packaging design should permit reuse (when specified) and recovery and should minimise the impact of packaging waste on the environment.

4   Automation in warehousing

Warehouse management systems (WMS)

4.1   WMS is a term used to refer to IT-based systems that integrate all aspects of stock management. As well as being used for forecasting and stock control, WMS can carry out the following functions.

- Recording receipts of items into the warehouse
- Updating stock records
- Allocating stock locations
- Preparing automated 'picking' lists. As mentioned earlier, these can be prepared to allow a forklift truck driver to proceed around the warehouse in a logical order. This avoids unnecessary movement and should greatly reduce the need for turning round and going back the way they have come. If this occurs, it is possible that the forklift truck will encounter other forklift trucks moving the other way. There is not usually room for two forklift trucks in one aisle and congestion is likely to occur.
- Designing effective storage and warehouse layout incorporating such factors as whether items are fast-moving or slow-moving; dangerous; requiring 'special' facilities such as cool storage, etc.

4.2   WMS can also be used as an interface with other departments such as Finance or Purchasing. Such systems may either be purchased 'off the shelf' or can be designed and tailored to suit the organisation's specific needs.

4.3   One area of warehouse management where WMS can be very useful is that of 'trade-offs'. These are comparisons of, for example, the service level that could be provided with different stock levels. The 'trade-off' aspect is that a lower service level would be provided with a lower stock level. However, if the stock level were increased to provide a better service level, the stockholding cost would be increased. The 'trade-off' is service level against cost of stockholding.

4.4   If such 'trade-offs' are to be contemplated, it is better to evaluate them on the basis of quantitative data rather than subjective 'feelings'. WMS can model different outcomes based on different situations: for example, if the level of stockholding were 'x', the resultant service level would be 'y'.

4.5   There are other types of 'trade-off' and the types of data necessary to carry out the modelling of warehouse and distribution systems would be as follows.

- Costs and lead times that would be likely to result from different numbers of warehouses. Having more warehouses might reduce lead times but would increase costs.
- Costs associated with different types of materials handling equipment and storage facilities. For example, drive-in racking might improve the use of warehouse space and make stock rotation and usage more efficient but might cost rather more than having ordinary adjustable pallet racking.
- Customer service targets: these might be based on matters such as how frequently individual

customers place orders as well as the typical order quantities from each customer. This type of information would be known as **customer ordering profiles**.

4.6 Customer ordering profiles change over time, as do transport networks. Any system selected must be able to adapt to such changes as well as to any other changes in the external environment. WMS should be able to model warehouse systems under different scenarios and simulate different outcomes based on changing situations.

4.7 Such systems should allow warehouse managers to compare their options and make decisions based on predicted outcomes relating to performance. An example of the need to consider different situations in order to be able to make a decision on an important aspect of warehousing might be the question of whether to operate from a number of regional distribution warehouses or from one central warehouse.

4.8 In the above scenario, factors that would need to be 'traded off' would include the following.

- Relative land and property costs between a number of regional locations and one central location. Such a comparison would vary depending on how many regional warehouses were being considered.
- The cost of multiple stockholdings (ie having to stock the same items in more than one place) relative to the cost of having one stockholding in a central location.
- The locations of the main customers. This assumes a relatively small number of large customers. If customers, generally, are of roughly the same size, their locations would be more relevant. The purpose of this is to know where warehouses should be located if the multiple option is chosen.
- Acquisition costs of delivery vehicles, whether by outright purchase or by lease or hire. Generally speaking, more vehicles would be needed in the central warehouse scenario.
- Operating costs of delivery vehicles per mile or kilometre. Again, many journeys are likely to be longer when made from a central warehouse.

4.9 In the above scenario, the WMS enables objective comparisons to be made and is therefore likely to lead to better decision making.

Information systems

4.10 Information and communications technology (ICT) is having a growing impact on storage and distribution operations. Current and developing communications tools are enabling faster, more accurate communication between organisational control and operatives. The external role of IT is becoming more important as organisations continue to link systems.

4.11 Stores and distribution personnel have greater demands placed on them than ever because of their role in supply chains and their interface with the customer. To operate effectively the warehouse requires a fast, flexible and accurate IT system with the ability not only to control operations and reporting within the warehouse, but also to provide required information to any number of outside users.

4.12 Control and information systems should perform the following tasks.

- Capture delivery information accurately
- Record stock movements
- Maintain stock balances
- Monitor productivity and utilisation

- Track the movement of goods through the system
- Sort order requirements into appropriate picking tasks

4.13 Information must be available at different levels within the organisation.

- **Top-level management** requires information for strategic and policy-planning decisions.
- **Middle management** requires information for tactical planning and decision-making.
- **Supervisors** require information for operational planning and control.
- **Operators** require information relating to deliveries, order processing, and enquiry response.

4.14 The typical storage and distribution system (as part of an integrated logistics system) must cope with a wide variety of customer demand. Some customers will order on a regular basis and in standard or unit load quantities, while others will be short-term, requiring an individual response. The system, particularly at operational level, needs flexibility and responsiveness to be built in.

4.15 Logistics system information must reflect the requirements of all levels. The central role of logistics within the company means that the system should coordinate the flow of materials through the entire system providing the right information, maintaining accuracy and helping deliver customer service.

4.16 New technology has led to major advances in the capabilities of information systems. Within logistics management, order processing, inventory and warehousing management, and vehicle management have all seen considerable developments allowing for a range of improvements.

- Enhanced speed of order entry and order processing can reduce lead-time.
- Warehouse planning and utilisation can be more cost-effective and improve customer service.
- Better management of inventory reduces delivery costs.
- Administration can be more accurate.

4.17 The stock management system should be designed to fulfil the above requirements, plus other criteria that may be demanded by individual organisations. The system also has a role to play in maintaining stock integrity by:

- Recording and identifying damage
- Identifying loss
- Recording deterioration
- Ensuring that stock rotation and specific environmental product needs are being met.

4.18 ICT provides a valuable logistic tool and has applications in key areas such as automatic stock control (re-order point), modelling of proposed changes to warehouses and operational processes, and vehicle tracking. If ICT is used well the storage and distribution operation can benefit from its application to business problems and issues. Efficiencies can be made by inputs from suppliers, production and manufacturing, demand management and other related areas that allow increases in flexibility and better planning in a way that was not possible only a few years ago.

4.19 The impact of ICT in warehouse operations has been impressive in recent years.

- Radio frequency identification discs (RFID) allow for more information on products to be captured by the stock management system. RFID systems are a significant advance on traditional barcoding.
- Electronic data interchange (EDI) allows the transfer of standardised or formatted data between buyer and supplier organisations.

- Increased computing power, the internet and increased use of emails have also benefited warehousing.

4.20 ICT can benefit the supply chain in a number of ways.

- Faster communications
- Information sharing
- Track and trace systems
- Direct ordering
- Streamlined administration
- Greater information gathering potential
- Closer links with suppliers and partners
- Inventory management

Chapter summary

- A unit load is a number of similar items or packages assembled into one batch.
- There are many types of racking, many of which are suitable for pallets.
- Some racking systems such as mobile racking and 'live storage' are designed to maximise the use of space.
- It is important that warehouse design and layout allows for good housekeeping, traffic flow, stock-picking and security as well as having provision for long-term flexibility.
- There are many different types of materials handling equipment such as pallet trucks and forklift trucks. Most of these are designed to carry pallets or other unit loads.
- Powered materials handling equipment allow much greater weights and volumes of items to be moved around the warehouse more quickly.
- It is important that items are packaged for protection and to facilitate handling and movement.
- Environmental considerations are also important in relation to packaging.
- Increasingly, warehouse and distribution operations are impacted by developments in ICT.

Self-test questions

Numbers in brackets refer to the paragraphs above where your answers can be checked.

1 Explain what is meant by unitisation and give two examples of it. (1.3)

2 Why might the use of forklift trucks mean that some space is wasted in the warehouse? (1.15)

3 Explain how live storage works and why it might be considered advantageous. (1.23–1.26)

4 What is the purpose of the 'counterbalance' on a forklift truck? (2.6)

5 List key considerations in the selection of handling systems and equipment. (2.16)

6 What are the main functions of packaging? (3.3)

7 What functions are typically carried out by a warehouse management system? (4.1)

8 In the context of warehousing and distribution, what types of information are needed at different levels in the organisation? (4.13)

9 List supply chain benefits that arise from ICT. (4.20)

CHAPTER 9

Transportation in Logistics

Assessment criteria and indicative content

3.1 Explain the main modes of transportation in logistics

- Defining logistics and transportation
- Modes of freight transportation: road, rail, air and sea
- Transport planning and modelling
- Reverse logistics

Section headings

1. Defining logistics and transportation
2. Sea freight
3. Air freight
4. Road freight
5. Rail freight
6. Transport planning and modelling
7. Reverse logistics

1 Defining logistics and transportation

Distribution

1.1 Distribution has been defined by the National Council of Physical Distribution Management as follows: 'Distribution is the efficient movement of finished product from the end of the production line to the consumer, and in some cases includes the movement of raw materials from the source of supply to the beginning of the production line. These activities include freight transportation, warehousing, materials handling, packaging, inventory control, plant and warehouse site selection, order processing, marketing, forecasting and customer service'.

1.2 The definition provides a checklist of the roles with which the distribution manager needs to be familiar in order to operate successfully. These areas are worthy of more consideration.

- Freight transport: by road, rail, sea or air, or a combination? Should an in-house vehicle fleet or a third-party provider be used?
- Warehousing: what should be the location, size, layout and purpose? Should the organisation's own warehouse or that of a third-party provider be used?
- Materials handling: what storage, racking, conveyors, forklift trucks, communications and accessibility systems should be used?
- Packaging: issues such as splitting and re-packing, pick and pack areas, packing suitable for purpose and costs should be considered.
- Inventory control: what options relating to warehouse stock control, location control, use of technology and integration with other business requirements, (MRP, DRP, ERP etc) should be followed?

- Plant and warehouse site selection: they should be near customers, road and rail links, and staff; should they be bought, rented or leased, are they accessible and secure?
- Order processing: IT systems, administration systems, customer service implications, and links with other business functions should all be considered.
- Marketing: delivery is the physical link between the company and customers, so there should be emphasis on building customer relationships, and systems that allow delivery promises to be kept and returns to be handled effectively.
- Forecasting: getting the forecasting right means that the organisation ends up with the right size of warehouse, the right long-term location, the right size and type of vehicle fleet, the right mix of goods passing through the storage and distribution channel, and the right equipment to handle them.
- Customer service is the end result of all the other areas being carried out effectively.

1.3   It can be seen that distribution is a complex business area encompassing a wide variety of individual functions. It does, however, form only one part of the wider concept of logistics and the supply chain.

1.4   Distribution was once described by Michael J Baker as 'the Cinderella of marketing'. This view was based on the marketing mix concept of the 4 Ps of marketing – price, product, promotion and place – where distribution forms part of the place (delivery) element. Michael Baker felt that this element of the marketing mix had not historically been given the weighting and importance it deserved.

1.5   Events since then (including the downturn in trade in the early 1990s, increased global competitiveness, together with the impact of information technology) have elevated the role of distribution as organisations have worked toward cost reduction and gains in both efficiency and effectiveness. The role of distribution is now firmly integrated into the thinking of successful organisations and this role is being widened as organisations adopt more rounded logistics approaches.

1.6   Physical distribution is not only a cost, it is a potent tool in creating demand. Organisations can attract additional customers by offering better service or lower prices through distribution improvements.

1.7   The objectives of distribution are customer-focused: to provide the customer with an effective and efficient service by meeting delivery requirements in all respects. The main objectives for distribution are a blend of:

- meeting predetermined cost targets;
- providing a level of service that seeks to grow the business and raise the organisation profile and reputation in the market;
- contributing toward providing a reasonable profit margin.

1.8   The service level of distribution must be balanced against the level of costs incurred in meeting the customers' delivery requirements. Getting this balance correct, while also meeting both the profit needs of the organisation and the customer's needs, is a key consideration in distribution.

Logistics

1.9 The storage and distribution operation does not function in isolation. Storage and distribution forms an integral constituent of an organisation's logistics strategy. Logistics involves the movement of goods from source through to customer. This will normally involve raw materials, semi-manufactured goods, components and finished goods being controlled and managed by a number of different suppliers.

1.10 Logistics can be seen as complementary to supply chain management as the movement of goods underpins effective supply chain management. The logistics approach, particularly when sourcing internationally, may mirror the tiering approach of supply chain management in allowing each link in the supply chain to control its own storage and distribution requirement. However, owing to the complexities and responsibilities involved, an organisation may adopt a more strategic perspective and manage the movement of goods, in particular, in a more proactive way.

1.11 Logistics departments now appear on the organisation charts of most of the world's largest companies. This represents a radical change in the way of thinking within organisations, as implementation of a logistics strategy involves a reappraisal not only of business practices but also of business thinking.

1.12 Logistics has a number of definitions.

- 'The process of planning, implementing and controlling the efficient and cost-effective flow and storage of raw materials, in-process inventory, finished goods and related information from the point of origin to the point of consumption, for the purpose of conforming to customer requirements.' (*Management of Business Logistics*, Coyle, Bardi and Langley)
- 'The process of ensuring that the right products reach the right place in the right quantities at the right time to satisfy customer demand.' (Institute of Logistics and Transport)
- 'The process of strategically managing the movement and storage of materials, parts and finished inventory from suppliers, through the firm and onto customers cost-effectively.' (Martin Christopher)

1.13 It has also been defined even more succinctly as: 'The time-related positioning of resource.'

1.14 Let us consider one further definition offered by Richard Schonberger, which implies that just sufficient quantities should be made to meet immediate needs and that questions of quantity are closely related to questions of time. 'Produce and deliver finished goods just in time to be sold, subassemblies just in time to be assembled into finished goods, fabricated parts just in time to go into the subassemblies, and purchased materials just in time to be transformed into fabricated parts.'

1.15 We can think of logistics as management of the storage and movement of goods and information. Good use and implementation of logistics within an organisational strategy can cut costs, speed up work, provide a basis for improvements in effectiveness and efficiency and improve customer service.

1.16 Logistics involves the co-ordinated management of material and information flows throughout the organisation. Supply chain management deals with the same issues throughout the chain from sources to customers, with an emphasis on business and commercial aspects. Logistics and supply chain management are closely linked therefore. Logistics can be viewed as a strand running through all the traditional functions of the supply chain, from raw material sourcing through to delivery to the customer.

9

1.17 Key to logistics thinking is an appreciation of geography, time, space and value, that is the time that materials take to move and the quantity of material to be moved. If a JIT production system is in use this increases the frequency of deliveries and reduces the quantity per delivery, but the 'trade-off' is in better quality, no inventory and no warehouse.

1.18 The integration of logistics calls for companies to remove or reduce functional barriers (such as those between production, finance and marketing departments) to focus on a streamlined management process designed to meet increasing customer demands and the needs of a competitive marketplace. Hierarchical structures in particular do not suit a logistics approach.

2 Sea freight

Containerisation

2.1 The majority of goods handled internationally are transported by sea freight. The most notable development in the industry in recent years has been the advent of containerisation. Containerisation offers both benefits and disadvantages when compared with the more traditional between-deck/break-bulk stowage used in conventional vessels.

2.2 The advantages of containerisation are as follows.

- The introduction of door-to-door movements
- Increased security due to containment
- Reduced handling
- Improved transit and turnaround times
- Cost savings from areas such as packing and better space usage
- Improved service quality

2.3 The disadvantages of containerisation are as follows

- Huge initial investment in vessels, ports and facilities
- Costs of investing in, maintaining, tracking and storing containers
- Not all cargoes are suitable for containerisation

General features of sea freight

2.4 The majority of inter-continental freight moves by sea. Sea freight is often cost-effective when compared with other transport modes when the cargo is travelling over longer distances. Each ship follows a timetable and calls at several ports on each trip.

2.5 Sea freight offers three categories of shipping.

- **Deep-sea shipping** (referring to the depth of the ocean). Large container vessels and bulk-tankers of commodities such as iron ore, petroleum and grain move the majority of the world's trading goods.
- **Coastal shipping**. This has lost its dominant status as the pattern of trade has changed and the road network has improved. Coastal shipping used to involve the movement, primarily of commodities, around the coast. As the importance of commodity industries has declined, most notably the coal industry, this trade is of far less importance today. Oil and gas are moved by pipeline, reducing the need for a coastal support network.
- **Short-sea trades**. This term covers short sea journeys, often in the form of roll-on, roll-off (ro-ro) vessels operating to regular sailing schedules to established ports with a developed infrastructure and linked road network.

2.6   Shipping lines request that cargo is delivered two or three days before departure. This allowance must be added to the transit time. The door-to-door time will be longer than the port-to-port times advertised and this should be considered when customers are advised.

Containers

2.7   Containers are not delivered to the vessel but into inland clearance depots, which are designed to speed up clearance of both imports and exports while also relieving port congestion. Three types of related arrangements are container bases (CB), container yards (CY) and container freight stations (CFS) which offer facilities for storing, 'stuffing' (technical term for loading) and stripping containers.

2.8   Most sea-freight traffic is shipped in containers (often referred to just as boxes). They are used in two different ways.

- FCL (full container-load): a container with one load.
- LCL (less than container-load): an individual shipment forming part of a container-load. This is often referred to as groupage: a number of LCL shipments are grouped (usually by freight forwarders) with other shipments to form an FCL.

2.9   When loads are grouped to form an overall load they are known as **groupage shipments** (when using sea or road). When the equivalent happens for air freight the term applied is **consolidation**.

2.10   There is a range of container sizes available but the majority are constructed to an ISO (International Standards Organisation) specification enabling their use on an international scale. The basic sizes are 2.45m width, 2.60m height. They are usually made of steel or aluminium.

2.11   There are several types of container, the principal ones being as follows.

- General (dry) container: the most frequently used, this is suitable for most types of general cargo. It is fully enclosed and has end doors for access.
- Insulated and refrigerated containers: often referred to as 'reefers'. They are specially designed to cater for perishable cargoes, which need to be transported at low or frozen temperatures.
- Open top containers: designed to accommodate over-height cargoes or where the cargo needs to be loaded from above.
- Open-sided containers: suitable for cargoes more easily loaded from the side.
- Flat-rack containers: with panelled-in ends, these are suitable for over-width or over-height cargoes and will often be used for items such as machinery and vehicles.
- Half-height containers: these are suitable for particularly dense cargoes where weight is considerably greater in relation to the volume.
- Bulk powder (or liquid) containers: these are used for specialist cargoes such as fertilisers, wine and dangerous goods.

Evaluating whether to use sea freight

2.12   Sea freight offers a service that is cost-effective and, in most cases, reliable. For logistics managers there is a need to build in not only the transit times of the vessels but also time to allow for delivery, handling and customs clearance at each end of the transit. The attractiveness of sea freight can be evaluated as follows.

- **Cost**. For a large majority of goods ranging from commodities to manufactured goods, sea freight remains the lowest cost option particularly for those travelling long distances. Where speed of service is unimportant or has been built in to the logistics timing, sea freight remains very competitive.
- **Availability**. Vessel sailing schedules and types are published up to a year in advance particularly on the main international trading routes. This enables logistics managers to plan production and delivery schedules ahead of time and minimise costs.
- **Flexibility**. There is a wide range of vessels and vessel types ranging from specialist commodity carriers (grain, oil, etc) to tramp vessels available for hire as well as conventional vessels (where the goods are loaded in the hold) and container vessels.
- **Speed**. Vessels are not designed for high speed. They are designed to be fuel-efficient and they travel at the optimum speed to achieve that. They operate to a sailing schedule, so they can be used with a high degree of predictability, but vessels are subject to breakdown, the effects of bad weather and port congestion at times.
- **Handling**. Container vessels use technology extensively to locate containers in the appropriate position to allow for loading and offloading at ports. Vessel turnaround times are kept to a minimum by transferring cargo for loading from the ICD to meet the incoming vessel. As with any transport mode, costs are incurred when a vessel or vehicle is not moving, as it is not earning money. If conventional sea-freight methods are being used – eg if goods are packed in wooden crates and stowed in the hold of the vessel – the cargo will be subject to more handling than it would be if containers were used. This increases the risk of pilferage, damage and delays. 'Through' transport, which equally can involve containers, involves transfer from one vessel to another, again increasing the risks.

2.13 The main involvement of the logistics sector with sea freight is concerned with container traffic. Cellular container vessels typically carry between 2,000 and 6,000 TEUs ('20-foot equivalent units') and in future vessels are planned which will carry up to 8,000 TEUs. Modern container vessels are very sophisticated and maximise their use of technology. They are supported by booking systems, load planning and container location programmes that offer a high degree of professionalism.

3 Air freight

Characteristics of air freight

3.1 Air freight has also seen changes and developments particularly since about 1990. Passenger aircraft have increased in both number and size, which increases their capacity for freight as well as passengers. Technology has improved cargo storage, tracking and handling. Specialist freighter aircraft range from the Hercules (approximate 18-ton capacity) to the Boeing 707 (approximate 40-ton capacity) and the Boeing 747 (100-ton capacity) among others. However, the vast majority of air-freight consignments travel on passenger aircraft in the cargo holds.

3.2 This transport mode is used primarily for low-weight, low-volume, high-value goods where speed is a main consideration. Freight rates can be reduced by using the services offered by freight forwarders but often remain uncompetitive when compared with sea, road or rail.

3.3 Air-freight cargo is handled using integrated IT systems from booking through to delivery to the forwarder or airline and on through to the customer. 'Track and trace' systems allow both airlines and exporters to find out the location of cargo at any time. Proof of delivery now forms an integral part of the tracing network, allowing shippers to get real-time information on their consignments and delivery confirmation, if required.

3.4 Air-freight cargo is traditionally carried in the 'belly' of the aircraft. Unit load devices (ULDs) enable loads to be pre-built for direct loading into an aircraft. They are made of aluminium and are designed to fit specific areas of the aircraft belly. They are, in essence, containers for aircraft (although smaller and irregularly shaped to fit the rounded shape of aircraft).

3.5 Consolidation services (where individual shipments are grouped together to form a larger one) are offered by freight forwarders and are now the most common method of sending air-freight consignments. The freight forwarder books the entire load with the airline under the **master airwaybill** and issues **house airwaybills**, covering individual consignments, to shippers.

Evaluating whether to use air freight

3.6 The attractiveness of air freight can be evaluated as follows.

- **Cost**. Air-freight rates can be high when compared to sea freight but costs can be reduced by using the services of a freight forwarder offering consolidation services; by buying in bulk from the airline the forwarder can offer reduced rates to customers.
- **Availability**. Major international routes can be served many times daily. With more remote locations transhipment services are available to a wide range of locations.
- **Speed**. The main advantage of despatching goods by air rather than sea is speed, which comes at a price. Considerations that may favour air-freight despatch include value of the cargo, urgency, reduced packing and insurance costs and enhanced cashflow through faster delivery enabling quicker payment.
- **Handling**. Aircraft are limited in the size, weight and capacity of cargo they can carry. The majority of bulk cargo will be limited to sea freight for long distances.

4 Road freight

Introduction

4.1 International road haulage has developed greatly in recent years. Advantages offered by road transport are that goods can be carried on the same unit from door to door with industrial or warehouse facilities usually easily accessible by road.

4.2 Tractors (the engine and cab of a truck) can be used to carry a variety of 'trailers'.

- **Containers**
- **Tilt trailers**, where a tarpaulin cover encloses the goods and offers protection from the weather. Standard length is 13.6 metres with an internal width of 2.4 metres and a height of up to 2.5 metres. The 'tilt' is supported by wooden or metal supports, which remain fixed to the trailer but can also be easily removed to facilitate loading and unloading if required.
- **Draw-bar trailer** (also known as a 'road train'): an extended tilt trailer. The first part is the rigid vehicle and the second part is a trailer.
- **Box trailers**: where the carrying unit is a box with solid sides and doors. All sides are solid offering greater protection than may be the case with a tilt trailer. Loading is by the back doors. Box trailers are often used to transport fragile consignments such as computers, electrical equipment, etc.
- **Flat trailers** (also known as flat beds): standard trailers that do not have a tilt. Often used for

9

goods that, owing to their size or configuration, cannot easily be carried on a standard tilt trailer. Sheeting only lightly protects goods.

Evaluating whether to use road freight

4.3   The attractiveness of road haulage can be evaluated as follows.

- **Cost**. Costs are increasing as rising fuel costs, increasing restrictions on drivers' hours and congestion are all impacting on the industry. Increasing costs are being met by more efficient vehicles, effective route planning and better use of technology.
- **Availability**. Vehicles are often available at short notice and offer the ability to deliver door to door.
- **Speed**. Road haulage can offer door-to-door deliveries within a short timeframe. Haulage competes favourably with air freight where goods need initial transfer to an airport, loading, unloading, clearance and delivery whereas a direct road delivery can be made.
- **Handling**. By utilising a unitised (standard) load such as a container, handling can be restricted to loading and unloading the container. Goods can also be secured using 'groupage' services offered by freight forwarders and logistics operators when shippers do not have a full container-load. In addition, a driver will accompany the load, which aids security and can keep customers informed of the current status of the load.

4.4   Road haulage offers a number of advantages built around convenience and flexibility that other transport modes find it difficult to match.

- Door-to-door deliveries
- Responsive delivery availability
- Greater efficiency when compared with other transport modes in short- to medium-distance deliveries
- Reduced delays – with the benefit of telematics delays can be advised
- Security as loads can be secured at the point of loading and delivered intact accompanied by the same driver
- Reduced packing costs if goods are containerised or transited within a known handling network
- Documentation can be that of the consignor and is delivered with the goods
- Smaller consignments can be sent on groupage services with other consignments destined for the same geographic location and then on-delivered, at competitive cost.

4.5   Road transport is a highly regulated business area that requires specialist management. The road haulage industry has often been criticised, particularly on environmental concerns that are increasingly becoming an issue. The main criticisms put forward are as follows.

- **The creation of traffic congestion**. The industry itself suffers from this and tries to limit the impact. Vehicles are often scheduled for delivery outside main working hours, in-cab telematics can aid drivers in avoiding congestion spots, and route planning can take into account congestion bottlenecks.
- **Road haulage adds to the number of road accidents**. One repercussion of this view is the introduction of regulations to ensure that drivers do not work excessive hours and so fall asleep at the wheel. Vehicles also need to meet rigorous legal criteria to operate. This ensures that accidents caused by mechanical failure are reduced to a minimum.
- **Road haulage causes and adds to noise, vibration and visual intrusion**. Road designers are well aware of the problems caused in this area and design new roads accordingly, often with

screening, embankments or trees to help reduce the impact. Vehicle sizes are often subject to restrictions to minimise the effects on the general public and the road network.

- **Road haulage adds to pollution**, a social issue that the industry takes very seriously. There have been major advances in engine technology that have reduced fuel consumption while reducing pollution levels. Legislation in this area is very strict.

Ro-ro ferries

4.6 Ro-ro (roll-on, roll-off) is a method of transport where the tractor and trailer drive onto the ferry and drive off again at destination. The goods remain loaded on the vehicle throughout the crossing.

4.7 The routes offer a great deal of flexibility in terms of destination, with schedules published and known in advance. As the vast majority of cargo remains on the originating trailer delivery can be made door to door.

5 Rail freight

Introduction

5.1 Particularly in Europe and the USA, rail services are well geared to freight traffic and can offer a high level of service at competitive prices.

5.2 Rail cargo often consists of commodities or semi-manufactures and is carried in conventional wagons, special purpose wagons or swap-bodies. A recent growth area is the development of intermodal transport particularly involving transfer of containers from rail to road and *vice versa* (see later in this chapter).

Evaluating whether to use rail freight

5.3 The attractiveness of rail freight can be viewed as follows.

- **Cost**. Rail freight is highly competitive in terms of cost, often utilising the underused network at off-peak times. Rail offers the ability to move large volumes of freight, particularly to inland destinations, over large distances.
- **Availability**. This is restricted for most organisations because of the need to deliver to and collect from a railhead. This is increasingly being addressed by investment in multimodal services allowing for interchange between road and rail thereby permitting door-to-door deliveries at reduced cost.
- **Speed**. Although some door-to-door services are offered they are the exception rather than the norm. Generally speed would not be a priority. However, rail can be effective when delivering over long distances as restrictions that apply to vehicle drivers do not affect rail haulage.
- **Congestion**. Rail services remove vehicles from the road network.
- **Reduced pollution and energy consumption** when compared to road haulage. Direct links on a dedicated network and increasingly energy efficient locomotives add to rail's attractiveness to companies wishing to display their green credentials.
- **Dangerous goods movement**. Rail offers a proven safety track record over road.
- **Public safety**. Rail has an impressive safety record with deaths per 100 million vehicle kilometres much fewer than on the roads. Major incidents are investigated thoroughly and safety is now a major consideration.

5.4 However, rail has a series of limitations that restrict its ability to deliver the flexibility and convenience of road haulage, though the railway industry is being creative in developing solutions to meet modern business needs. The main disadvantages could be summarised as follows.

- **Lack of ability to offer direct deliveries**. Rail is restricted to movements to railheads (although dedicated handling areas and equipment plus a closer relationship with road when handling unit loads may be set to change perceptions in this area).
- **Inflexibility**, particularly for smaller consignments.
- **Lack of speed and adaptability** required for just in time systems.
- **Specialised wagons limit handling**. A constraint that applies in many countries is the height of the rail wagon owing to the number of low bridges.

5.5 A growing area of traffic comes from intermodal swap-body traffic, loaded onto rail at ICDs from road vehicles and reloaded at a convenient point to facilitate door-to-door delivery.

6 Transport planning and modelling

Introduction

6.1 Vehicle routing and load planning will vary considerably from company to company. Channels of distribution (delivery to retailers, warehouses, factories, etc), vehicle suitability, congestion (and congestion charging), loading and unloading facilities, and a host of related factors make routing and planning individual to particular organisations. However, there are common considerations that apply across the board.

6.2 As part of distribution planning considerable thought will be given to the mix of vehicles required and their purpose. This planning will address how the distribution function meets the strategic goals of the organisation and will consider the key areas of:

- warehousing (in-house or outsourced)
- vehicles (own fleet, mixed with outside company provision or subcontracted to a third party).

6.3 The decisions made relating to the two key factors will establish the direct importance of vehicle routing and planning to an organisation. By outsourcing, the role is passed on to a third party provider but if the role is kept in house then vehicle routing becomes a key role in fleet management.

The factors to consider in vehicle routing

6.4 A wide range of factors must be taken into account when planning delivery tactics and operations. These will involve the collection and collation of data together with information relevant to tactical and operational aspects.

- Demand data. This is a business area that has witnessed dramatic improvements by leading organisations in recent years. Accuracy of demand figures reduces waste and cost and the area has been the subject of increasing application of both stand alone and integrated software systems that aid in projecting future demand.
- Time and distance factors. These areas underpin vehicle routing and planning but are often the result of a prior decision of where to locate a factory or warehouse. Time and distance factors would have been included as part of this evaluation but delivery needs will still need to be met.
- Route factors involve the different types of roads, congestion, changing situations (that can be met by contingency planning and communicated via telematics).

- Customer and service constraints which need to be met in order to attain organisational objectives.
- Vehicle limitations and restrictions and how to work effectively (eg by using a third party provider).
- Driver constraints, particularly following regulations on maximum working hours.
- Product and unit load constraints and how to optimise resources around these key criteria issues.

6.5 Demand data is particularly relevant as it can represent the main measure of vehicle capacity. It will include such variables as:

- weight (per product type delivered, total delivery weight)
- cube (volume – the space occupied by the freight)
- unit loads, roll cages or pallets
- location including postcodes or zipcodes.

6.6 Time and distance factors link in with the issue of warehouse or depot location discussed in earlier chapters. The more distant the warehouse from the delivery points the greater the time taken to deliver. This is a generalisation of course, as road links, congestion and delivery time will all also influence the final time taken.

6.7 Distance measurements have traditionally been taken using maps to estimate the true distance. This has largely been superseded by the impact of IT and telematics (the use of on-board electronic systems).

6.8 With regard to IT, software programmes have become increasingly effective as the size, speed and memory of computers have increased and costs have fallen. Software packages are available to enable route planning supported by contingency planning in the case of accidents or delays *en route*, together with planned stop periods and driver speed estimates.

6.9 Telematics allow for vehicle tracking via global positioning satellites (GPS) and communication with the driver by mobile phone or by fax. As with many cars, digital maps are available in-cab.

6.10 Route factors will involve considering the delivery implications of specific routes together with compatibility to make other deliveries, if required. This may mean collation of orders to a specified geographic area on particular times and days in order to utilise the vehicle effectively. This may have an impact on customer service.

6.11 Customer service implications must be fully considered during the delivery planning process.

- Suitable delivery times
- Whether collection is required
- Access or parking restrictions
- Early closing days
- Drop-size limitations

6.12 Vehicle limitations and constraints involve the planner in considering the types of vehicles available and their suitability to meet delivery criteria. This can include vehicle type, capacity and size, and involves the factors mentioned under customer service implications above. Using the right vehicle for the right delivery increases efficiency and minimises costs.

6.13 Driver constraints will involve examining the following issues.

- Driver scheduling and availability
- Work hours
- Licensing
- Training required to drive certain vehicles
- The possible need for a mate to help with the delivery

6.14 Product or unit-load constraints have a big influence on delivery planning. Weights, dimensions and volume (cube) affect handling and may increase the need for specific loading and unloading equipment. The product may need segregating on the vehicle because of its hazardous nature or the risk of tainting (smell being passed from one product to another, eg clothes smelling of paraffin). Variable delivery times for mixed loads may be needed. Unit loads may be needed; although they offer security, convenience and protection, they require specialist equipment.

Vehicle scheduling and routing systems

6.15 Vehicle scheduling and routing represent yet another trade-off between efficiency in delivery and customer service expectations. Success is achieved by meeting customer service targets within budgeted cost parameters. Points to be considered when examining a system designed to achieve this would include the following.

- **Type of system**. Fixed or flexible routes; day or flexible planning; fixed vehicles or flexibility built-in; regular pattern of driver delivery or adjustable according to customer needs.
- **Standards of operation**. There should be an objective standard for: the driver's work; optimum routes used; speeds for specific types of roads; driver knowledge when calling and collecting; presentation of driver; start and finish times.
- **Routing**. This should address the trade-off between efficiency levels (vehicle capacity, drivers' hours, etc) and customer service levels in order to maximise potential.
- **Scheduling**. This should aim to attain the best use from vehicles and drivers: one journey or more; avoiding congestion periods (travel on a motorway at 4am to see how vehicle scheduling works); booking systems; using the correct vehicles for the job in hand.
- **Type of vehicle**. The correct size and type available to suit delivery factors; use of contract vehicles, if required.
- **Contingency planning**. Know what contingencies are likely to cause delay by keeping, recording and analysing reasons for delay; build in alternate routes, vehicles and solutions to plans.
- **Control and responsibility**. Measure performance of drivers, vehicles, loading and unloading time and other relevant factors; compare against targets; take action if performance targets are not being met. Ensure individuals have responsibility for these areas together with checking schedules and the ability to alter schedules if the circumstances require it. The control system must allow flexibility.

6.16 The areas of vehicle scheduling and route planning are complex ones requiring sound long-term planning backed up by a flexible and proactive operational aspect. The aim should be to meet customer needs within budgeted constraints.

Telematics

6.17 Telematics can be defined as:

- 'Electronic systems which communicate between car (vehicle) and road, to optimise traffic flow, aid navigation and avoid collisions.'
- '... vehicle tracking, navigation and real-time driver information.'

6.18 A further, more comprehensive definition was given in an Institute of Logistics and Transport special interest group report on opportunities for the application of telematics in a multi-site operation, as follows.

- 'Telematics is the in-cab information system equipment which enables the logistics operator to manage the fleet, by knowledge of where the vehicles are and when; how well they are being driven; and how well they are performing.'

6.19 The report examined the role of on-board systems and, in particular, their role in delivering added-value benefits. It stated that data communications and office management systems can prove the ultimate transportation resource, offering benefits such as better, faster customer service, greater competitiveness, improved safety and security, and reduced administration and costs.

6.20 Telematics represents the merging of electronic technologies in a manner that aids communication, aids route planning and contingency planning by being able to offer and communicate alternatives (eg a different route if a motorway is blocked), and enables monitoring of the vehicle fleet. Telematics is a tool that aids the fleet manager in meeting the day-to-day operational requirement and in the more tactical requirement of monitoring routes, costs and usage.

Steps in vehicle routing

6.21 CIPS suggest that the following steps are needed to achieve efficient routing.

- Establish delivery date and parameters
- Determine geographic data
- Determine demand
- Determine customer drop constraints
- Allocate demand to geographic area
- Decide on geographic rules
- Plan trips
- Plan routes
- Calculate vehicle requirements and mileage
- Calculate delivery costs
- Calculate vehicle utilisation

Global positioning satellites (GPS)

6.22 The Global Positioning System (GPS) is a satellite-based navigation system made up of a network of satellites placed into orbit by the US Department of Defense. GPS was originally intended for military applications, but in the 1980s the government made the system available for civilian use. GPS works in any weather conditions, anywhere in the world, 24 hours a day. There are no subscription fees or setup charges to use GPS.

6.23 GPS satellites circle the earth twice a day in a very precise orbit and transmit signal information to earth. GPS receivers take this information and use triangulation to calculate the user's exact location. Essentially, the GPS receiver compares the time a signal was transmitted by a satellite with the time it was received. The time difference tells the GPS receiver how far away the satellite is. Now, with distance measurements from a few more satellites, the receiver can determine the user's position and display it on the unit's electronic map.

6.24 Telematic systems have developed very quickly in recent years. The use of GPS systems in cars is now commonplace. It is equally commonplace when operating a vehicle fleet. GPS can be extended in use to give the fleet operator up to date positional information and connectivity with vehicles on the road via the internet and using mobile communications.

6.25 Fleet tracking systems use satellite technology to provide real-time locations and to record historical vehicle activity. They can bring a number of business benefits.

- Increase productivity. The system can help eliminate inefficiencies and save workforce time. This enables better vehicle utilisation increasing the productive work that vehicle and driver can carry out.
- Reduce labour costs. Eliminate discrepancies between hours worked and hours claimed by drivers with computer generated timesheets.
- Control fuel costs. Reduce the overall fuel bill with vehicle activity reports and fuel card integration. Eliminate unapproved or extended journeys.
- Improve customer service by reaching customers faster or at the agreed time on a more consistent basis.
- Increase fleet safety and security. With real-time GPS vehicle tracking vehicles can be constantly monitored.
- Operating costs can be reduced as GPS vehicle tracking drives out inefficient management practices. The new discipline forces managers to re-evaluate their working methodology.
- Reduces carbon footprint and improves environmental position while saving money on fuel.
- Reduce or eliminate unauthorised use of vehicles

6.26 Applications driving the increase of factory-fitted telematics include emergency calling, stolen vehicle tracking, and internet access. In-vehicle internet access could lead to a wide range of interesting new services. Examples include weather reports or parking information for the driver's destination, remote diagnostic information or even having emails read aloud while driving.

Transport modelling

6.27 Transportation forecasting is the process of estimating the number of vehicles and people that will use a road, bridge, railway, supermarket, airport etc, over a defined period of time. This traffic data is combined with other known data, such as population, trip rates, employment levels, travel costs etc, to develop a traffic demand model.

6.28 Traffic forecasts are used extensively in developing transportation policy, planning and engineering: to calculate the capacity of an infrastructure, to project the number of lanes a bridge should have or to route the traffic around busy urban areas, to estimate the financial and social viability of a project.

6.29 The classical urban transportation system model examines the process in four steps.

- Trip generation, which determines the frequency or origins and destinations of trips in each zone by trip purpose, as a function of land uses, household demographics and other socio-economic factors
- Trip distribution, which matches origins with destinations, often using a gravity model function
- Mode choice, which examines the proportion of trips between each origin and destination that utilises a particular transport mode
- Route assignment, which allocates trips between an origin and destination by a particular mode to a route.

6.30 After the classical model assessment, there is an evaluation according to an agreed set of decision criteria and parameters. A typical criterion is cost-benefit analysis which might be applied after the network assignment model identifies needed capacity.

6.31 Computer based transport modelling provides a means of showing what happens when different travel parameters are implemented in a range of scenarios. This process is often modelled using computer simulations, as this enables relatively quick manipulation of data to create alternative scenarios in a cost-effective manner. Using these scenarios, it is possible to make an educated guess as to what factors will affect future patterns of travel.

6.32 A transport model is a mathematical representation of an area of a transport system which can be used to evaluate existing conditions and project future effects brought about by changes due to traffic growth and/or infrastructure or land-use developments. Models can be as simple as a manual distribution of predicted traffic flows, but more often involve the use of specialised computer programs so that, for example, large geographic areas, complex interactions or a range of demand responses can be assessed.

6.33 Traffic modelling generally requires real-time or near real-time results. The main challenges to developing effective models relate to the availability of data and the business-case for development. Journey time prediction is one key factor addressed by transport modelling in a fragmented market. Others would be journey time reliability, incident response, environmental modelling including emissions, medium and long-term modelling.

7 Reverse logistics

The concept of reverse logistics

7.1 The traditional view of logistics management is that it is concerned with the movement of raw materials from the point of origin through the supply chain and on to the customer cost-effectively. The chain is balanced by a flow of forward and reverse information based on customer orders, forecasting and safety margins that enable the development of a balanced operation. However, there are instances when goods flow in the opposite direction. This is called 'reverse logistics', and it is an area that is coming under increasing scrutiny by companies as they seek to improve their customer service offering and gain from the return of usable stock to their managed inventory.

7.2   A definition is given by David Hughes in his article 'Reverse Thinking in the Supply Chain' (*Logistics Focus*, September 2003):

'Reverse logistics is the process of moving goods, packaging, equipment and information back from the point of sale, in counter flow to the forward supply chain. The objective is to minimise the on-cost of handling, while maximising the value from the goods or correct disposal. The key requirement is to speed up this cycle.'

7.3   The definition highlights the need for a process to enable reverse logistics to take place. Cost minimisation is a driver in making this process workable and will require a system-supported approach. Perfect stock should be returned to inventory for resale at full price. Perfect stock in damaged packaging should be repackaged and resold at full price.

7.4   Reverse logistics has a wide remit and return traffic covers a variety of different situations.

- Goods returned, as they are faulty, damaged or fail to meet customers' expectations
- Product recall for quality or safety reasons
- Unwanted or surplus goods
- Pallets, roll cages and other unit load devices being returned after use
- Used packaging being returned for recycling or disposal

The first three on the above list are often interlinked.

7.5   The reverse supply chain is difficult to implement as it deals with low volume on an irregular basis, often scattered across a wide geographical area. The question that has traditionally been asked is 'does the cost of securing returns make the operation worthwhile?' The answer (with a few exceptions such as mail order companies) has been no, but changes are now taking place in the business environment that are forcing organisations to consider returns more seriously.

- More retailers are offering a no-quibble returns policy to customers.
- Customers are becoming more likely to return products – both as faulty and with no fault.
- Customers are more aware of their rights to return goods.
- Internet selling and the growth in home delivery encourage and increase returns if the product fit is not as expected.
- Environmental legislation is forcing recycling of products and packaging.
- Hazardous materials require special handling and disposal.
- Disposal of waste electrical and electronic equipment (WEEE) could cause end-of-life products to be returned to the retailer.

Methodology in reverse logistics

7.6   With regard to stock management reverse logistics will involve putting in place practices and procedures:

- to collect surplus or unrequired stock from customers and return it to stock;
- to repair damaged but repairable items;
- to repack stock that has damaged, irrelevant or out-of-date packaging.

7.7   Returns on an increasing scale, through changes in customer actions, recall needs or the increasing intrusion of legislation, are clearly making reverse logistics an integral part of the logistics operation.

7.8 Returns from shops and warehouses represent one of the larger growth areas that reverse logisticians need to consider. At retail policy level, returns are open to abuse or fraud and the opportunity for this abuse to take place must be minimised. Returns and the reasons for return should be recorded to identify patterns of consumer behaviour, faulty goods or other identifiable reasons.

7.9 David Hughes gives a number of reasons for returns.

- Over-merchandising
- Poor ordering
- Promotional stock pushed into shop
- Customer warranty returns
- Bulk product recalls, unfit for sale
- Damaged packaging or damage in transit
- Wrong delivery
- End-of-season ranges, end of promotion, end of sale
- Change of display
- Stock-counting forcing a clear-out or discovery of lost stock
- Badly bought goods, slow sellers
- Dead or dormant stocks
- Salvage from sun damage, fire, flood
- Out of date, past its 'best before' date, obsolete
- Reallocation, branch-to-branch transfers
- Return to inventory

7.10 The financial cost of returns to organisations can be substantial. Minimisation of many of the reasons highlighted above should be an acknowledged role of management. The application of technology can help, but clearly organisations should develop strategies not only to handle reverse logistics but also to minimise the reasons why returns are occurring.

7.11 Determining a strategy for handling the reverse flow of materials in a system is a prerequisite in ensuring that reverse logistics will operate effectively. This process will often need a change of thinking from both logistics managers and operatives, and good change management is required to demonstrate the advantages to be gained for the organisation overall.

7.12 Targets should be set and returns recorded against those anticipated. As more information and data becomes available, resources can be more effectively controlled and managed. Responsibilities should be clearly allocated to ensure systems work as anticipated and have flexibility built in to meet the diverse return needs that may occur.

7.13 Costs should be identified. Rushton, Croucher and Baker place the costs involved in product recall under four headings: communication costs, documentation costs, replacement costs and disposition costs. The authors attribute this list to John Gattorna's 1990 work, *Strategic Supply Chain Alignment*.

7.14 **Communication costs** include:

- registered and certified mail
- return receipts
- instructions
- telephone, faxes and emails
- messenger service.

7.15 **Documentation costs** include:

- filing of receipts of notices for recall
- estimates for disposition and replacement
- plans for replacement item
- instructions for replacement or repair
- authorisations for work to be performed
- receipts for items replaced or repaired.

7.16 **Replacement costs** include:

- manufacture and installation
- employee visits
- shipping, packing and warehousing
- testing and re-testing
- identification of product
- temporary personnel
- invoicing
- overtime of employees.

7.17 **Disposition costs** include:

- locating all items
- inventory of items
- removal from customers' property
- packaging and unpacking
- labelling
- shipping
- inspection
- repair and replace
- discard or salvage
- instruction pamphlet
- refunding
- allowances for time used
- repurchase of item
- compensation for loss of use
- warehousing storage.

7.18 The benefit of returns should be balanced against these costs. Return of usable stock to inventory together with management approaches to identifying and reducing returns may, over a period of time, work toward a cost balance.

Product recall

7.19 The urgency of the product recall should also be considered. If goods are found to have been tampered with then speed may be of the essence. Having established the urgency the goods must be located. They could be anywhere within the distribution channel. The more complex the distribution channel the more complex the problem. Good record-keeping and use of technology through a traceability system can help in the search. If goods have been sold to the public, product recall notices may need to be advertised in the local or national press.

7.20 Assuming goods are located they must be returned. This can be an expensive and difficult exercise. Consumers may need their costs recompensed. Retailers may not be geared up to serve as recall centres. Goods must be collated at a central point and may require to be held in isolation from other products. Associated transport and storage costs will be higher than standard costs.

7.21 Individual organisations should consider whether this is an area they can effectively handle in house or whether control can be outsourced to specialist providers.

KPIs for reverse logistics

7.22 Appropriate key performance indicators (KPIs) include return rates, actual costs, costs net of recovered costs, and time.

Chapter summary

- Storage and distribution forms an integral part of an organisation's logistics strategy.
- Logistics involves the storage and movement of goods and information.
- Sea freight is widely used where speed is not a major consideration. Containerisation is an invariable feature of sea freight.
- Air freight is speedy but expensive. It is normally used for low-volume, high-value items.
- Road freight offers the benefit of door-to-door delivery. Unit loads, often containers, are an important feature.
- Rail freight is becoming more popular as rail companies develop multimodal services.
- Transport planning is a major element in efficiency and cost reduction.
- Reverse logistics has become a major issue for many organisations. As the frequency of returns increases, businesses need to develop systematic methods for dealing with them.

Self-test questions

Numbers in brackets refer to the paragraphs above where your answers can be checked.

1 Define distribution. (1.1)

2 Define logistics. (1.12)

3 What are the advantages of containerisation in sea freight? (2.2)

4 What factors affect the attractiveness of air freight? (3.6)

5 List advantages of road freight. (4.4)

6 List criticisms of road freight. (4.5)

7 What factors will typically be considered in planning vehicle routing? (6.4)

8 Define telematics. (6.17)

9 What are the four typical steps in a process of transport modelling? (6.29)

10 In what situations does a need for reverse logistics arise? (7.4)

11 List reasons why returns occur. (7.9)

CHAPTER 10

Transport Documentation

Assessment criteria and indicative content

3.2 Explain documentation that relates to transport in logistics

- Common transit procedure
- TIR carnet
- Uniform Customs and Practice for Documentary Credits and letters of credit
- Packing list, waybill, consignment notes, bill of lading
- Certificate of origin
- Single administrative document
- Electronic documents

Section headings

1 Imports and exports within the EU
2 Letters of credit
3 Documents in international trade
4 Electronic documents

Introductory note

Although this unit is part of a global qualification, certain topics in this area of the unit content appear to refer specifically to transport within the European Union. This is the case for 'common transit procedure' and 'single administrative document'. At the time of writing (June 2012) it is not clear whether candidates from other areas of the world will be expected to show knowledge of these specific EU issues, or whether questions will be framed on a more global basis.

1   Imports and exports within the EU

The common transit procedure

1.1 The Single Market Act was introduced in 1986 and led to the introduction of the single European market in January 1993. The Act introduced the 'four freedoms' to the European Union, on areas where there had previously been restrictions on free flow.

- People
- Capital
- Services
- Goods.

1.2 The free movement of goods is designed to ensure that goods that are of 'European Union origin' (ie which have been manufactured in the EU or which have had import duty paid upon import into the EU, often referred to as 'Community goods') are deemed to be in 'free circulation' (duty only needing to be paid once) and have 'Community status'. (The term 'Community' refers to the

European Community, the former name of the European Union.) To support the single market the customs tariff was harmonised across EU member countries so that the same import duties and quotas apply over every member country.

1.3 Goods are divided into two categories.

1 Those that have Community status ('Community goods'). These are goods that:
- originate in the European Union
- have been imported from a non-EU country and are in 'free circulation'. The term 'free circulation' is used to describe imported goods where all import formalities have been complied with and any customs duties have been paid. You only pay import duties once into the EU; the goods are then in 'free circulation' if moved to other EU countries.

2 Goods without Community status. These are goods which are from outside the EU on which no duty has been paid and no import formalities complied with. These goods are subject to Community Transit and Common Transit procedures.

1.4 Community/Common Transit is a Customs procedure that allows goods not in free circulation to move within the EU and EFTA countries. (EFTA is the European Free Trade Association. Its members are Iceland, Liechtenstein, Norway and Switzerland.) While under this procedure the payment of any customs duties is suspended. The external (T1) procedure is used for non-Community goods on which import duties have not been paid and the internal (T2) procedure is used for goods, not in 'free circulation', that are transiting from one EU member state to another through an EFTA country or moving overland to an EFTA country.

1.5 Goods transiting EU countries require a 'movement document'. Goods may be in free circulation, or they may be transiting through the EU to a destination outside the EU without being in 'free circulation', or they may have excise duty yet to be paid (eg cigarettes, alcoholic drinks) as examples. Community Transit (CT) is a Customs procedure, that allows goods not in free circulation to move within the EU. When under the procedure the payment of any customs duties is suspended.

1.6 The 'movement documents' are more commonly known as 'T-forms'.

TYPE OF T-DOCUMENT	USE	COPY OF SAD REQUIRED
T1	Where the goods are not in 'free circulation' within the EU	1, 4, 5 and 7
T2	Where the goods are in 'free circulation' within the EU	1, 4, 5 and 7
T2L	For 'free circulation' goods but where the 'community transit' (CT) system is not required	1 and 4

1.7 It is not necessary for a T-form to accompany the goods, only that the appropriate status is declared on the SAD form. (The SAD form is explained below.) However, if goods are moved under the full 'community transit procedure' the T-form must accompany them. This means that an import entry cannot be made to Customs prior to arrival of the goods, as is increasingly common practice with import entries. This will cause delays as Customs process the entry, since the T-form will need to be presented at the appropriate import office.

1.8 Goods that meet the criteria of 'free circulation' can now be moved freely within Europe without attracting duties and quota restrictions (restrictions by weight or number), although customs and excise authorities throughout Europe require evidence as to the status of goods while they are in transit and upon arrival. The effects of these changes are as follows.

- Goods moving from the UK to European member countries are no longer classified as exports but are now officially referred to as 'despatches'.
- Imports from European member countries into the UK are now referred to as 'acquisitions'.
- Goods that are in 'free circulation' and are transported between European member countries are no longer subject to Customs procedure but are still required to evidence their status with either an invoice, a transport document or a completed 'Copy 4' of the SAD form. Customs authorities always have the right to investigate the status further if they feel there is a need.

The Single Administrative Document (SAD)

1.9 The SAD form was introduced as the result of the 'Customs 88' project, which was designed to harmonise a wide range of customs documentation in different business areas into one form. It was introduced to simplify documentation, facilitate trade and allow for computerised communications throughout the European Union.

1.10 In its full eight-copy format the SAD form is intended to be used as a combined export, community transit and import document. However, traders are not required to present all eight copies in every circumstance. SAD sets are available containing only those copies that are appropriate. These sets are known as 'split sets' and, as an example, may be used when goods are transiting through Europe or when goods are being exported.

1.11 The SAD form is usually issued in eight-part sets (with variations for Common Agricultural Policy and other specific areas). The complete form is used for declarations for exports and imports from non-EU countries. Within the EU only the following copies are required.

COPY NO	DESCRIPTION OF COPY	LOCATION OF COPY
1	Copy from customs office of departure	Despatch (export) country
3	Consignor/exporter's copy	Despatch (export) country
4	Copy for the customs office of destination or EU status (T2L declaration)	Travels with goods
5	Return copy from customs destination office to evidence arrival	Travels with goods; returned to despatch country as evidence of arrival
7	Statistical copy in country of destination	Travels with goods

1.12 The SAD form sounds a complex document but becomes familiar with use. Its purpose is:

- to allow customs to monitor the movement of goods;
- to ensure all relevant duties have been paid;
- to ensure regulations, such as statistical declaration, have been complied with (statistical information is required to show balance of trade and industry trend information among other purposes).

New Computerised Transit System (NCTS)

1.13 The New Computerised Transit System (NCTS) is a European wide automated system to enter declarations electronically and is designed to provide better control of goods in European Union and European Free Trade Area (EFTA) transit. NCTS encompasses 29 countries in total.

1.14 NCTS works by a customs declaration being delivered in an electronic way to customs authorities. Following acceptance the declaration gets a unique registration number. The goods will then be released and can be moved, accompanied by the customs document, to the place of destination.

10

Meanwhile the Customs office of departure sends details of the consignment to the office of arrival. After checking and acceptance the goods will be released and confirmation passed back to the office of departure.

1.15 NCTS was introduced as a result of a European Parliament enquiry into transit fraud and is seen as an essential element intended to make the transit systems more secure. The enquiry found that the existing paper based systems were open to fraud and incapable of providing a reliable level of management and control of goods in transit.

1.16 All organisations that use Community/Common Transit can use NCTS. The objective is that all traders will input all transit declarations and other details such as arrival of goods to NCTS electronically. Connected traders will receive electronic responses advising of decisions during the procedure such as acceptance of the declaration, release of goods etc, at both departure and destination.

1.17 For organisations the NCTS brings the following advantages.

- An improved quality of service with less waiting time at HMCE and greater flexibility in presenting declarations
- Speedier control and release of goods at the office of destination
- Reduction in costs, time and effort when compared to the paper based system
- The opportunity to integrate electronic transit declaration procedures with an organisation's existing computerised system
- Greater clarity and consistency in requirements

1.18 The New Computerised Transit System (NCTS) processes traders' electronic customs transit declarations. It is mandatory for traders using Community and Common Transit to make their declarations using the NCTS, which is used by all the member states of the European Union and the European Free Trade Association (EFTA) countries.

2 Letters of credit

2.1 A letter of credit (also referred to as a documentary credit) is a guarantee of payment made by a bank to a named beneficiary, guaranteeing that payment will be made provided the stipulated terms of the letter of credit have been complied with.

2.2 Using letters of credit is essential in certain countries in international trade, and exporters and importers need a reasonable understanding of how they work. However, the procedure is somewhat complex and to help your understanding it is worthwhile to bear in mind what the system attempts to achieve.

- For the seller, the aim is to ensure payment without recourse to litigation, especially since such litigation might involve a foreign jurisdiction. Preferably, the seller would like the source of funds to be located in his own country.
- For the buyer, the aim is mainly to ensure that payment is not made until he has received assurance that the goods have been transferred to himself.

2.3 These aims are achieved by the use of two banks as intermediaries: one in the seller's country (the advising bank), and one in the buyer's country (the issuing bank). In brief, the buyer instructs the issuing bank to open a credit with the advising bank in favour of the seller. The seller will be able to draw on this credit – ie obtain funds from the advising bank in his own country – once he has delivered to the advising bank any documents specified by the buyer, such as a clean bill of lading.

2.4 Having paid the seller, the advising bank passes on the documents to the issuing bank and is reimbursed for the sum advanced. The issuing bank in turn presents the documents to the buyer in return for payment. The end result is that the buyer has paid, and the seller has received, the contract price, while the intermediary banks have received fees for handling the transaction.

2.5 The seller will invariably insist that a confirmed irrevocable letter of credit is used.

- 'Confirmed' means that the advising bank has confirmed the arrangement with the seller in its own country, and the seller therefore has confidence in receiving funds from a local source once he has delivered the required documents.
- 'Irrevocable' means that the issuing bank receives an irrevocable authority from the buyer, and also undertakes irrevocably to act on that authority. This means that the issuing bank must honour the credit, even if the buyer attempts to revoke the agreement (as might happen, for example, if some dispute arose between buyer and seller).

2.6 The banks involved in this transaction act as agents of the buyer, and they run the risk that he, as principal, will refuse to ratify their actions. This he might do, for example, if the documents tendered to him do not comply with the requirements that he laid down. To protect themselves against this possibility, banks will normally refuse to accept documents from the seller unless they comply in every respect with the buyer's stipulations.

2.7 Use of letters of credit is by no means a fail-safe system. In particular, the number of parties involved can mean that delays arise. It can happen, for example, that goods arrive at the port of destination before the buyer has received the bill of lading from the issuing bank. The carrier will be reluctant in that case to hand over the goods. In practice, the buyer may persuade him to do so by indemnifying him against any loss he may suffer as a result.

2.8 Despite this kind of difficulty, the letter of credit is a central feature of modern international trade and you should ensure that you are familiar with the main principles. Note that most of the main banks issue useful booklets explaining the principles. For example, an exceptionally clear booklet entitled *Letters of Credit* is published by HSBC. It includes the very useful diagram reproduced in Figure 10.1 which summarises the procedures already described.

10

Figure 10.1 *Letters of credit flowchart*

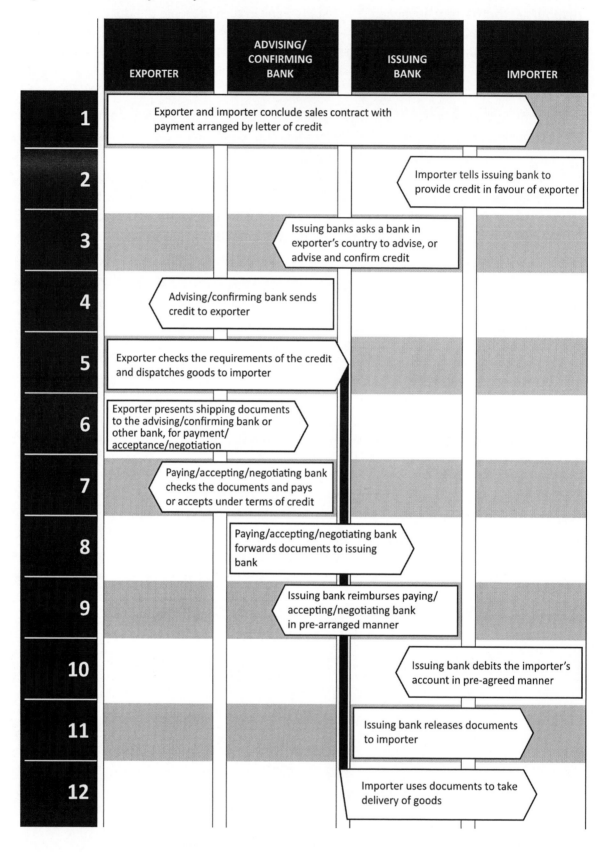

Uniform Customs and Practice for Documentary Credits

2.9   Trading internationally involves risks that are not present in domestic trade. Exporters run the risk of buyers failing to pay for goods, while importers may risk paying but never receiving anything. Owing to the distances involved, as well as legal and cultural issues, it may be difficult to resolve any disputes. The letter of credit offers a guarantee to the seller that they will be paid, and the buyer can be sure that no payment will be made until they receive the goods.

2.10   An international set of rules (Uniform Customs and Practice or UCP) governing the rights and obligations of traders and banks under letters of credit is produced by the International Chamber of Commerce. The current edition is UCP 600 (the successor to UCP 500) which came into force on 1 July 2007.

2.11   The purpose of UCP 600 is to standardise terms and procedures and to avoid misunderstandings in connection with letters of credit. The UCP standards give definitions of important terms that are used in letters of credit. When referring to letters of credit, banks and others involved in international trade will generally use the UCP definitions of key terms and phrases.

2.12   UCP 600 also sets out general documentary requirements and standard practices for handling letters of credit.

2.13   As UCP 600 standards are internationally recognised it is obligatory to use letters of credit that are covered by them. If a letter of credit is subject to UCP it will be stated on the letter of credit. It might include a statement such as 'This Letter of Credit is subject to the latest version of Uniform Customs and Practice 600 for Documentary Credits published and updated by the International Chamber of Commerce'.

2.14   In some instances the definitions and procedures set out in the UCP standards may differ from the laws of a particular country. However, adopting UCP 600 into the trading contract ensures that the courts will apply the rules governing UCP 600.

3   Documents in international trade

Invoice

3.1   The invoice is a commercial document issued by a seller to the buyer, indicating the products, quantities, and agreed prices for products or services the seller has provided to the buyer. An invoice indicates that the buyer must pay the seller, according to the payment terms (eg 60 days from invoice date).

3.2   The invoice is a formal request for payment from a seller to a buyer. In international trade it is also a document required by Customs authorities to provide evidence of value for statistical and other purposes and for Customs at the importing country who may levy import duty on the goods being imported.

3.3   Invoices in international trade are usually SITPRO-aligned which is an international standard for the layout of documents. The standard format aids the electronic transfer of information. The SITPRO alignment is common to many of the major documents used in international trade.

Packing list

3.4 A packing list shows packing details of a consignment. It is important not only for the customer but also for Customs authorities at both export and import points. If the consignment is examined it will first be checked against the packing list. If a discrepancy is noticed it is likely that the Customs authorities will investigate further.

3.5 At times this is required to comply with the specific terms of a letter of credit or with the regulations of an importing country.

Air waybill

3.6 An air waybill is sometimes referred to as an air-freight consignment note. It is not a document of title to the goods, nor is it transferable or negotiable. It is in essence a receipt for the goods and represents *prima facie* evidence of the conditions of carriage.

3.7 The standard IATA air waybill is used worldwide, IATA being the International Air Transport Association. The air waybill is a contract of carriage at departure airports. It also provides a point of reference and logging for inventory control. It includes a full description of the goods and full customs rating information. It will also highlight any special handling arrangements for the goods in transit.

3.8 When the goods arrive at the destination airport the air waybill provides a basic document for notification to the consignee, customs clearance and onward delivery to the consignee. Additionally it becomes the source document for accounting for clearance and delivery charges.

Bills of lading

3.9 The bill of lading is a vital document in international trade where sea carriage is the preferred mode of transportation. A bill of lading is customarily regarded as a receipt issued by the ship owner to the shipper (usually the exporting company or seller). The receipt covers:

- the quantity of the goods received
- the condition of the goods when received
- marks which clearly identify the goods.

3.10 A bill of lading generally contains the terms of carriage. However it should be noted that a bill of lading is only evidence of a contract of carriage if the holder of the bill is the shipper. It is only after a bill of lading is issued and made out to a third party, ie a consignee or endorsee, that the bill of lading becomes the contract of carriage.

3.11 A bill of lading is processed once the shipper or his nominated agent is advised of the sailing schedules. He will then contact an appropriate ship owner and book cargo space on the ship or container.

3.12 When the goods are on board the ship the bill of lading is signed and dated. Generally this is undertaken by the ship's master or his nominated agent and endorsed 'freight paid' or 'freight payable at destination'.

3.13 If all is well with the consignment the bill of lading will be signed without endorsement (a clean bill of lading). If otherwise, ie there is something wrong with the consignment, the bill of lading will be signed but endorsed with the appropriate comment making it an unclean or claused bill of lading.

Sea waybill

3.14 A sea waybill is a non-negotiable document consigned to a named consignee and does not need to be presented to secure title of the goods at the port of destination. It is effectively a 'received for shipment' document with an option for use as a shipped document. The shipper inserts the name of the contracting carrier to be used.

3.15 The document allows for the earlier release of the goods if received for shipment and thereby reduces delays associated with negotiability. It speeds the flow of goods to the consignee. A sea waybill is the preferred choice between multinational companies trading with each other.

Certificate of origin

3.16 The certificate is an important shipping document which specifies the quantity together with the value and place of manufacture of the goods being shipped. It is completed by the supplier of the goods and is authenticated by the chamber of commerce or other authorised body in the seller's country.

3.17 The main details on the certificate are as follows.

- Name and address of the exporter (generally the seller)
- Name and address of the importer (generally the buyer)
- Description of the goods
- Country of origin of the goods
- Signature accompanied by stamp or seal of the certifying body

3.18 Certificates of origin are not required by all importing countries. They are particularly important when transacting with Middle Eastern countries.

CMR consignment note

3.19 The CMR is a consignment note with a standard set of transport and liability conditions, which replaces individual businesses' terms and conditions. It confirms that the carrier (the road haulage company) has received the goods and that a contract of carriage exists between the trader and the carrier. It is a road haulage consignment note which conforms to the CMR Conditions of Carriage. When used it shows acceptance of these Terms and Conditions.

3.20 Unlike a bill of lading, a CMR is not a document of title nor a declaration, although some countries regard it as such. It does not necessarily give its holder and/or the carrier rights of ownership or possession of the goods, although some insurance is included.

3.21 A range of information needs to be covered in the CMR note.

- The date and place at which the CMR note has been completed.
- The name and address of sender, carrier(s) and consignee (the person to whom the goods are going).
- A description of the goods and their method of packing. The description should be acceptable to the consignor and consignee. For security reasons, we do not always want the carrier to be able to identify valuable goods.
- The weight of the goods.
- Any charges related to the goods, such as customs duties or carriage charges.
- Instructions for customs and any other formalities such as dangerous goods information.

10

TIR carnet

3.22   Carnets are important in the movement of goods internationally. A carnet is a permit or a form of licence designated for a particular purpose, usually temporary importation for a specific purpose such as film equipment, equipment for trade fairs and exhibitions, and equipment for sporting events. The import can then be taken into a country or it can be permitted to transit through a country without payment of any duties that would otherwise be due. This is subject to full documentary requirements being met and evidence of the goods leaving the country concerned.

3.23   TIR carnets are used to accompany goods travelling in sealed road vehicles and/or containers across many countries, as long as those countries are signatories to the United Nations TIR Conventions. Using this method avoids the requirement to complete national transit forms for each country through which the goods will travel. TIR is an abbreviation for *Transports Internationales Routiers*. The guaranteeing associations in each participant country issue these carnets.

4   Electronic documents

4.1   Logistics and transportation is a document-intensive industry. Manually processing these documents is a costly and time-consuming process. Companies are looking individually and/or as part of a wider supply chain to see how they can improve their operation strategies and reduce the amount of paperwork while increasing efficient shipping and timely delivery of their products.

4.2   General logistics trends include the increasing use of information technology (IT) and e-commerce, globalisation and companies increasingly paying attention to sustainability. The trends in sea freight are related for example to growing vessel size, trade imbalance, and increasing cost control and service level.

4.3   One of the major problem areas facing logistics management is the handling of documentation. Many documents can be produced and transferred electronically. These will facilitate the movement of goods, assist record keeping and enable tracking of shipments.

4.4   Document automation (also known as **document assembly**) is the design of systems and workflow that assist in the creation of electronic documents. These include logic based systems that use segments of pre-existing text and/or data to assemble a new document. This process is increasingly used within certain industries to assemble legal documents, contracts and letters. Document automation systems can also be used to automate all conditional text, variable text, and data contained within a set of documents.

4.5   Automation systems allow companies to minimise data entry, reduce the time spent proofreading, and reduce the risks associated with human error. Additional benefits include savings due to decreased paper handling, document loading, storage, distribution, postage and shipping, faxes, telephone, labour and waste.

Advance shipping notice

4.6   An advance shipping notice (ASN) is an advance notice of delivery. It is usually sent in an electronic format and is a common EDI document. The ASN can be used to list the contents of a shipment of goods as well as additional information relating to the shipment, such as order information, product description, physical characteristics, type of packaging, markings, carrier information, and configuration of goods within the transportation equipment. The ASN enables the sender to describe the contents and configuration of a shipment in various levels of detail and provides an ordered flexibility to convey information.

4.7   The ASN is noteworthy in that it is a new concept in logistics, enabled by the advance of modern communication methods. Although it provides information similar to the bill of lading, its functions are very different. While the bill of lading is designed to accompany the goods when shipped, the purpose of the ASN is to provide information to the destination's receiving operations well in advance of delivery.

4.8   The advantages to the logistics operation lie in four main areas: cost; accuracy; flexibility; and advance notification to Customs authorities.

4.9   The ASN can be used to pay suppliers directly for goods received. This can be accomplished by receiving the ASN into the company computer system, printing company labels for each container received, affixing the labels on the containers, and then transmitting any discrepancies to the supplier via EDI.

4.10 Electronic documents play a big role in the handling of these details, providing a means for better communications between manufacturers, distribution centres, shippers, transportation carriers, and other industry players.

IATA e-freight initiative

4.11 The International Air Transport Association (IATA) e-freight initiative has the objective of designing a system that will facilitate the paperless delivery of goods from shipper to consignee.

4.12 The IATA e-freight initiative aims to:

- Replace air carriage paper documents with electronic documents
- Use electronic data to eliminate paper air waybills (numbering in the hundreds of millions per year)
- Increase data quality, timeliness and consistency through Message Improvement Programme
- Automate Customs reporting (this will require some legislative changes)

4.13 Launched in 2007 it is intended to produce a paper free air cargo supply chain. Documents are to be replaced with the exchange of electronic data. The e-freight project needs to consider, amongst other things, local regulations, e-customs programs in place in individual countries and gaining support from relevant authorities and stakeholders.

4.14 By the end of 2011, 42 locations thoughout the world were operating e-freight, 109 major airports were live and 20 agreed standards were operating. Overall e-freight penetration was 11.14% of the market with a target of 15% by the end of 2012.

4.15 This final point serves to demonstrate the complexity of these projects and the time required to make them operational and get them embedded into working practices. Documentation may not be the most exciting subject in the world but advances in the way documentation is managed are crucially important for both the supply chain and logistics.

10

Chapter summary

- In the EU, goods are divided into two categories: Community goods and goods without Community status.
- A key document relating to the movement of goods in the EU is the single administrative document (SAD).
- A letter of credit is a vital method of payment in international trade. An advising bank in the seller's country guarantees payment to the seller; an issuing bank in the buyer's country guarantees not to pay on the buyer's behalf until all required documents have been received.
- Common documents in international trade include invoices, packing lists, air waybills, bills of lading, sea waybills, certificates of origin, consignment notes, and TIR carnets.
- International transportation is a document-intensive industry. Increasingly, this is tackled by means of automation and electronic documents.

 ## Self-test questions

Numbers in brackets refer to the paragraphs above where your answers can be checked.

1   What are the 'four freedoms' introduced in the European Union? (1.1)

2   What is meant by the Community Transit procedure? (1.4)

3   Describe the New Computerised Transit System. (1.13ff)

4   What are buyers and sellers trying to achieve in using letters of credit? (2.2)

5   What is meant by a 'confirmed, irrevocable' letter of credit? (2.5)

6   Explain what is meant by (a) a bill of lading and (b) a certificate of origin. (3.9, 3.16)

7   What is an advance shipping notice (ASN)? (4.6)

8   What are the aims of the IATA e-freight initiative? (4.12)

CHAPTER 11

Incoterms

Assessment criteria and indicative content

3.3 Assess common types of incoterms in international logistics

- The role of the International Chamber of Commerce
- The development of incoterms
- Classification of terms – E, F, C and D terms
- Rules for sea and inland waterway transport

Section headings

1 The role of the International Chamber of Commerce
2 Classification of incoterms
3 Rules for sea and inland waterway transport

1 The role of the International Chamber of Commerce

1.1 The ICC (International Chamber of Commerce) represents the voice of world business championing the global economy as a force for economic growth, job creation and prosperity. As national economies are now so closely interwoven, government decisions have far stronger international repercussions than in the past. The ICC seeks to highlight the needs of business on an international scale.

1.2 ICC activities cover a wide spectrum, from arbitration and dispute resolution to making the case for open trade and the market economy system, business self-regulation, fighting corruption or combating commercial crime. ICC provides business input to the United Nations, the World Trade Organisation, and many other intergovernmental bodies, both international and regional.

1.3 The ICC has direct access to national governments all over the world through its national committees. The organisation's Paris-based international secretariat feeds business views into intergovernmental organisations on issues that directly affect business operations.

Setting rules and standards

1.4 Arbitration under the rules of the ICC International Court of Arbitration is on the increase. Since 1999, the Court has received new cases at a rate of more than 500 a year.

1.5 The ICC has a major role in developing internationally agreed rules and standards that companies adopt voluntarily and can be incorporated in binding contracts. We have already seen UCP 600, governing letters of credit. And in this chapter we will be looking at another ICC publication, *Incoterms 2010*.

ICC and incoterms

1.6   The ICC originally published the very first set of incoterms in 1936. Since that first publication, they have been updated in 1953, 1967, 1980, 1990 and 2000 and most recently in 2010. *Incoterms 2010* came into force on 1 January 2011. They are now reviewed every ten years to ensure that they keep up to date with current trade practices.

1.7   When ICC first introduced the Incoterms® standard commercial terms in 1936 they represented a radically new way of thinking in the international business world. The new terms were the first real attempt to bring coherence to a commercial and judicial system that diverged widely from one country to another.

1.8   Incoterms (**In**ternational **Co**mmercial **Terms**) were introduced with the purpose of ensuring that international commercial transactions should be successfully completed within the concept of incoterms. It was felt that if the parties concerned in an international transaction adopted incoterms when making their contract then many problem areas could be avoided, as the parties concerned would both be clear on their areas of risk and their responsibilities.

1.9   Incoterms are standard definitions used in contracts to reduce confusion and avoid traders having difficulty understanding the import requirements and shipping practice used in other countries.

1.10   There is no legal requirement to use incoterms when drawing up an international commercial contract. However, if the parties adopt incoterms into their contract they are agreeing to be bound by the detailed specifications laid out in *Incoterms 2010*.

Incoterms 2010

1.11   Since the last revision of incoterms in 2000, much has changed in global trade. Cargo security is now at the forefront of the transportation agenda for many countries. In addition, the United States Uniform Commercial Code was revised in 2004, resulting in the withdrawal of the independent US shipment and delivery terms. The latest version of the incoterms rules will reflect these changes and others.

1.12   For business terminology to be effective, phrases must mean the same thing throughout the industry. Incoterms are designed to create a bridge between different members of the industry by acting as a uniform language they can use.

1.13   Although the adoption of incoterms into a contract will mean that courts will imply the standards of incoterms in law, the ICC will arbitrate on disputes. This will often prove a cheaper option than going to law. If this course of action is considered worthwhile the ICC recommends inclusion of the following term in the contract: 'All disputes arising in connection with the present contract shall be finally settled under the Rules of Conciliation and Arbitration of the International Chamber of Commerce by one or more arbitrators appointed in accordance with the said Rules'.

2 Classification of incoterms

2.1 Sending goods from one country to another as part of a commercial transaction can be a risky business. If they are lost or damaged, or if delivery does not take place, then the climate of confidence between the parties involved may degenerate to a point where legal action is considered. However, the sellers and buyers in international contracts inevitably want their contracts to be successfully completed. The use of *Incoterms 2010* can assist in achieving this objective.

2.2 Incoterms is a set of contractual conditions or terms that can be adopted into international contracts and which are designed to be understood and interpreted correctly on a worldwide basis. Terms of trade define the risks and responsibilities of buyers and sellers in the sale and delivery of goods to overseas markets. Defined in *Incoterms 2010* they represent a set of internationally agreed and widely accepted trade terms that are used by the vast majority of trading nations.

2.3 Each incoterm establishes who is responsible for costs and risks such as transport costs, insurance, duties payable and customs clearance. Incoterms are accepted by governments, legal authorities and businesses worldwide for the interpretation of most commonly used terms in international trade.

2.4 This reduces or removes uncertainties and often costly misunderstandings arising from different interpretation of such terms in different countries. Incoterms apply to both domestic and international sale contracts.

2.5 Incoterms continue to enable traders to make clear who is responsible for the goods at each point of the transport process in buyer or seller contracts.

2.6 The new incoterms will operate as follows.

Any mode of transport
EXW – Ex Works
FCA – Free Carrier
CIP – Carriage and Insurance Paid
CPT – Carriage Paid To
DAP – Delivered At Place
DAT – Delivered At Terminal
DDP – Delivered Duty Paid

Sea and inland waterway transport (only)
FAS – Free Alongside Ship
FOB – Free On Board
CFR – Cost and Freight
CIF – Cost, Insurance and Freight

2.7 The 2010 revision reduced the number of categories from four (E, F, C and D terms) to two categories (Terms for any mode or modes of transport, and Terms for sea and inland waterway transport). However the use of the old approach remains particularly useful in understanding how the export price builds up with the increasing incoterm being used: Figure 11.1.

Figure 11.1 *The basic concept of incoterms*

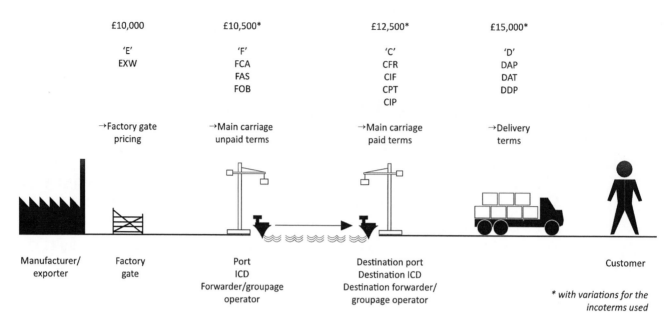

2.8 The above diagram illustrates where the various incoterms sit in the international movement of goods. EXW is in the seller's country, terms beginning in F are in the seller's country, terms beginning with C move the goods through to the importer's country and the terms beginning with D are in the importer's country.

2.9 Incoterms are best viewed and understood from the exporter's perspective. EXW (Ex Works) places the risk, responsibility and cost with the buyer as they have ownership of the goods when they leave the exporter's premises. As the goods move progressively nearer the importer the risk, responsibility and cost move according to the incoterm used. The final incoterm DDP (Delivery Duty Paid) leaves the exporter to cover all costs of delivery to the importer's premises.

'E'	Goods are made available to the buyer on departure at the exporter's premises
'F'	Goods are made available to a carrier appointed by the buyer. Main carriage is unpaid.
'C'	The seller pays for carriage but without assuming the risk for loss or damage to the goods after shipment. Main carriage is therefore paid.
'D'	The seller bears all costs and risks to bring the goods to the country or premises of the buyer.

EXW (Ex Works)

2.10 One of the simplest and most basic shipment arrangements, this places the minimum responsibility on the seller with greater responsibility on the buyer. The buyer bears all costs and risks involved in taking the goods from the seller's premises to the desired destination.

2.11 In an Ex-Works transaction, goods are made available for pickup at the seller's factory or warehouse and delivery is accomplished when the merchandise is released to the consignee's freight forwarder. The buyer is responsible for making arrangements with their forwarder for insurance, export clearance and handling all other paperwork.

2.12 This term requires the least effort by the seller, but should not be used where the buyer cannot carry out export formalities, when FCA or FAS may prove more appropriate. This term can be used across all modes of transport.

FOB (free on board) ... named port of shipment

2.13 FOB is one of the most common incoterms quoted and is suitable for conventional cargo.

2.14 Under FOB the seller has responsibility for delivering to the port or vessel nominated by the buyer. The responsibility and risk remain with the seller until the goods have been loaded on board the vessel nominated by the buyer. Cost and risk are divided when the goods are actually on board of the vessel (this rule is new). FOB can only be used for sea and inland waterway traffic.

2.15 FOB means that the shipper or seller uses his freight forwarder to move the merchandise to the port or designated point of origin. Though frequently used to describe inland movement of cargo, FOB specifically refers to ocean or inland waterway transportation of goods. Delivery is accomplished when the shipper/seller releases the goods to the buyer's forwarder. The buyer's responsibility for insurance and transportation begins at the same moment.

2.16 The seller must clear the goods for export. The term is applicable for maritime and inland waterway transport only but not for multimodal sea transport in containers. The buyer must advise the seller of the details of the vessel and the port where the goods are to be loaded, and there is no reference to, or provision for, the use of a carrier or forwarder. This term has been greatly misused over the last three decades ever since *Incoterms 1980* explained that FCA should be used for container shipments.

FCA (free carrier) ... named place of shipment

2.17 In this type of transaction, the seller is responsible for arranging transportation, but he is acting at the risk and the expense of the buyer. Where in FOB the freight forwarder or carrier is the choice of the buyer, in FCA the seller chooses and works with the freight forwarder or the carrier. Delivery is accomplished at a predetermined port or destination point and the buyer is responsible for insurance.

2.18 This term is replacing FOB in areas such as multimodal, container and through transport ('roll on, roll off' or ro-ro), and for delivery to airports. It is recommended for all modes of transport to a specific carrier or specific destination.

2.19 FCA means that the seller fulfils his obligation to deliver when he has handed the goods over, cleared for export, into the charge of the carrier named by the buyer at the named place. If no precise point is indicated by the buyer, the seller may choose within the place or range stipulated where the carrier shall take the goods into his charge. When the seller's assistance is required in making the contract with the carrier the seller may act at the buyer's risk and expense.

2.20 The seller retains responsibility and risk until the goods have been handed over at the named place or point.. This term, introduced in the 1990 revision, is suitable for all transport modes but is particularly relevant for airfreight or sea freight containerised transport.

2.21 A further clarification was introduced in *Incoterms 2000* to enable 'FCA ... seller's premises' where the risk transfers when the goods are loaded. This change was to address a weakness in EXW where the goods are made available but without being loaded. This use of EXW proved impractical in many situations.

2.22 The seller's obligation under FCA is to hand over the goods cleared for export, into the charge of a carrier named by the buyer at a named place or point. This term can be used for all modes of transport.

FAS (free alongside ship) ... named port of shipment

2.23 Here the seller must place the goods alongside the ship at the named port. The seller must clear the goods for export. The term is only suitable for maritime transport but not for multimodal sea transport in containers. This term is typically used for heavy-lift or bulk cargo where loading costs may be substantial.

2.24 In these transactions, the buyer bears all the transportation costs and the risk of loss of goods. FAS requires the shipper or seller to clear goods for export, which is a reversal from past practices. Companies selling on these terms will ordinarily use their freight forwarder to clear the goods for export. Delivery is accomplished when the goods are turned over to the buyer's forwarder for insurance and transportation in the seller's country.

CFR (cost and freight) ... named port of shipment

2.25 With CFR the seller undertakes and bears the expense of delivering goods from his premises to the port of destination, However, the risk of loss or damage to the goods, and other costs relating to events after the goods are delivered on the vessel, are transferred to the buyer when the goods pass over the ship's rail at the port of shipment, so the cost of marine insurance is borne by the buyer.

2.26 This term defines two distinct and separate responsibilities. One is dealing with the actual cost of merchandise 'C'. The other ('F') refers to the freight charges to a predetermined destination point. It is the seller's responsibility to get goods from their door to the port of destination. Delivery is accomplished at this time. It is the buyer's responsibility to cover insurance from the port of origin or port of shipment to buyer's door. Given that the shipper is responsible for transportation, the shipper also chooses the forwarder.

2.27 The term is suitable for sea and inland waterway traffic, as CPT could prove more accurate for container or through transport. The seller is required to provide all export documents: certificate of origin, export licence, pre-shipment inspection certificates, etc. if required.

2.28 The seller must pay the costs and freight required in bringing the goods to the named port of destination. The seller is required to clear the goods for export. This term should only be used for sea or inland waterway transport.

CIF (cost, insurance and freight) ... named port of shipment

2.29 This arrangement is similar to CFR, but instead of the buyer insuring the goods for the maritime phase of the voyage, the seller will insure the merchandise. In this arrangement, the seller usually chooses the forwarder. Delivery, as above, is accomplished at the port of destination.

2.30 This term is similar to CFR with the addition that the seller arranges marine insurance to protect the goods for the benefit of the buyer against loss or damage to the goods during carriage. Since it is the seller who enters into the contract of insurance he may choose the minimum level of insurance. The buyer may require a higher level and this should be clarified when drawing up the sales contract.

2.31 The seller is required to clear the goods for export. This term should only be used for sea or inland waterway transport.

CPT (carriage paid to) … named place of destination

2.32 CPT was one of the new terms introduced in the 1990 revision of incoterms and, as such, has been designed to suit the needs of modern business. The term is used primarily for traffic moved by container (including airfreight containers) or any multimodal method.

2.33 CPT specifies a named place; the relevant risks are transferred to the buyer on delivery to the designated place. The precise place should be considered when drawing up the sales contract. With CPT the seller is responsible for arranging and paying for the transit to the named destination.

2.34 The seller pays the freight for the carriage of goods to the named destination. The risk of loss or damage to the goods occurring after the delivery has been made to the carrier is transferred from the seller to the buyer. This term requires the seller to clear the goods for export and can be used across all modes of transport

CIP (carriage and insurance paid to) … named place of destination

2.35 This term is similar to CPT with the addition that the seller must purchase insurance. As it relies on the carrier's insurance, the seller is only required to purchase minimum coverage. When this particular agreement is in force, freight forwarders often act in effect as carriers. The buyer's insurance is effective when the goods are turned over to the forwarder.

2.36 The seller has the same obligations as under CPT but has the responsibility of obtaining insurance against the buyer's risk of loss or damage of goods during the carriage. The seller is required to clear the goods for export but is only required to obtain insurance on minimum coverage. This term requires the seller to clear the goods for export and can be used across all modes of transport.

DAT (delivered at terminal)

2.37 This term is used for any type of shipments. The seller pays for carriage to the terminal, except for costs related to import clearance, and assumes all risks up to the point that the goods are unloaded at the terminal.

2.38 Seller delivers when the goods, once unloaded from the arriving means of transport, are placed at the disposal of the buyer at a named terminal at the named port or place of destination. Both parties should agree the terminal and if possible a point within the terminal at which point the risks will transfer from the seller to the buyer of the goods.

2.39 The seller is responsible for the costs and risks to bring the goods to the point specified in the contract. The seller should ensure that their forwarding contract mirrors the contract of sale. The seller is responsible for the export clearance procedures. The importer is responsible to clear the goods for import, arrange import customs formalities, and pay import duty.

2.40 If the parties intend the seller to bear the risks and costs of taking the goods from the terminal to another place then the DAP term may apply. This term is a new introduction in the 2010 revision.

11

DAP (delivered at place)

2.41 DAP term is used for any type of shipments. The seller pays for carriage to the named place, except for costs related to import clearance, and assumes all risks prior to the point that the goods are ready for unloading by the buyer.

2.42 The seller delivers the goods when they are placed at the disposal of the buyer ready for unloading at the named place of destination. Parties are advised to specify as clearly as possible the point within the agreed place of destination, as risk transfers at this point from seller to buyer. If the seller is responsible for clearing the goods, paying duties etc, then consideration should be given to using the DDP term.

2.43 Under DAP the seller bears the responsibility and risks to deliver the goods to the named place and is required to clear the goods for export. The seller is responsible for delivering the goods to the named place in the country of importation, including all costs and risks in bringing the goods to the import destination. The importer is responsible for effecting import customs clearance and paying any duties and fees.

DDP (delivered duty paid)

2.44 DDP term tends to be used in intermodal or courier-type shipments. The seller is responsible for dealing with all the tasks involved in moving goods from the manufacturing plant to the consignee's door. It is the seller's responsibility to insure the goods and absorb all costs and risks including the payment of duty and fees.

2.45 DDP represents the ultimate extension of responsibility as a supplier. The seller arranges for the entire undertaking from despatch to final delivery, bearing all the main costs. The advantage to buyers is that they know exactly what they are paying, particularly if quoted in local currency. The main disadvantage to the seller is that capital costs are tied up until payment is received.

2.46 DDP is the opposite of EXW as it represents the maximum obligation that can be imposed under incoterms on the seller. If the seller cannot obtain an import licence this term should not be used. DDP is suitable for all transport modes.

2.47 The use of incoterms in a contract can save pages of detailed negotiation as, when adopting incoterms into the contract, the detailed specifications relating to the relevant incoterm will apply, defining areas of risk and responsibility. Areas detailed within incoterms specify the obligations of buyer and seller in regard to, among other things:

- where delivery should be made
- who insures
- what level of insurance is required
- who raises particular documents.

Applying incoterms to a contract

2.48 When applying incoterms to an international sales contract the buyer must be sure that the correct term is used to suit the circumstances. Although negotiation of the right term, from a commercial point of view, is important to the discussion it must also be borne in mind that there is a direct relationship between the choice of transport mode and the choice of delivery term.

2.49 *Incoterms 2010* reflect changes in business, particularly the growth in containerisation, unit load devices and multimodal and intermodal shipments. The terms FCA, CPT and CIP were introduced in the last two revisions enabling parties to nominate a point that suited their needs and which does not necessarily have to be linked to an airport or port.

Applying incoterms to a seafreight consignment

Figure 11.2 *Build-up of costs for the buyer using incoterms*

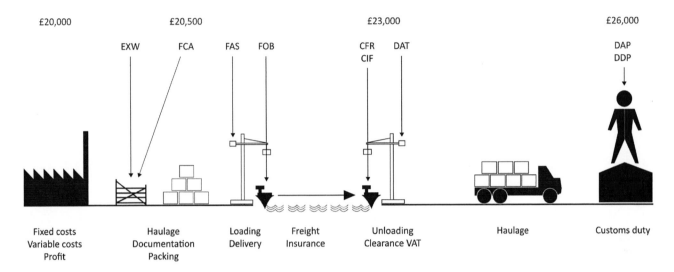

2.50 The above diagram illustrates how the price quoted by the exporter will increase as an incoterm used brings the goods closer to the importer. For example, with EXW the goods only have to be made available at the exporter's premises while for CPT the exporter needs to cover freight, insurance and other charges to a named place in the importer's country. The exporter will need to recoup the money laid out by increasing the price of the goods.

2.51 Figure 11.2 examines incoterms applicable to a sea freight consignment. Any approach to incoterms should be viewed from the exporter's perspective. The incoterm and the costs involved build up until they reach DDP, offering the highest cost to the exporter and highest level of service to the customer.

2.52 Figure 11.2 indicates a generalisation of the price applicable and costs involved for the 'E', 'F', 'C' and 'D' delivery. However these prices and costs will differ between for example FCA and FAS, as the place where risk and responsibility pass are at different points. For example, FCA could involve delivery to an inland clearance depot while FAS will incur additional transport and administration costs from the depot to the port of shipment.

3   Rules for sea and inland waterway transport

3.1 Terms of trade define the risks and responsibilities of buyers and sellers in the sale and delivery of goods to overseas markets. Defined in *Incoterms 2010* they represent a set of internationally agreed and widely accepted trade terms that are used by the vast majority of trading nations.

3.2 *Incoterms 2010* have been the result of considerable detailed work by the ICC and the new rules illustrate the need to be current and up to date in international trade issues. Of particular relevance were the points below.

- Adaptation of the rules to reflect (and better to fit) their use in practice in domestic as well as international trade, as well as within trade blocs such as the European Union where many border formalities have fallen away.
- Recognition of electronic means of communication, where the parties agree, or where this is customary – albeit without any detailed provisions covering particular electronic communications practices.
- Insurance cover – revisions to take account of alterations made to the Institute Cargo Clauses, and clarification of the parties' insurance obligations.
- Security – allocation of responsibility to obtain or to render assistance in obtaining security-related clearances, such as chain-of-custody information.
- Avoidance of potential double charging of terminal handling costs to the buyer by clear allocation of responsibility for such costs.

3.3 *Incoterms 2010* divides terms under two headings.

- Terms for any mode of transport. These consist of the following seven terms: EXW, FCA, CIP, CPT, DAP, DAT, DDP.
- Rules for sea and waterway transport. These consist of the following four terms: FAS, FOB, CFR, CIF.

3.4 With the majority of international trade travelling by water it is important to have a good understanding of the second category in particular. Purchasers need to understand *Incoterms 2010* when buying internationally in order to be certain what they are agreeing to when negotiating or forming a contract.

3.5 The rules for sea and inland waterway transport have a similarity in that the point of delivery and the place to which the goods are to be carried are ports.

Incoterms summary

3.6 The International Chamber of Commerce recommends using *Incoterms 2010* after year 2011. However, according to the ICC, parties to a contract of sale can agree to use any version of *Incoterms*. All contracts made under the previous version of *Incoterms* remain valid even after 2011.

3.7 In international trade it must be assumed that your supplier fully understands incoterms. When importing there is a clear need to understand where risk and responsibility pass and which party is obligated to which precise point. If you are involved in using incoterms the *Incoterms 2010* publication issued by the International Chamber of Commerce is essential.

Chapter summary

- The ICC performs a wide range of activities in the promotion and regulation of international trade.
- The ICC publishes *Incoterms 2010*, the most recent edition of incoterms.
- The latest incoterms are arranged in two categories: those suitable for any mode of transport, and those suitable only for transport by sea and inland waterway.
- Each incoterm lays down responsibilities for buyer and seller. These are expressed in terms that are understandable internationally, reducing possible misunderstanding between buyer and seller.

Self-test questions

Numbers in brackets refer to the paragraphs above where your answers can be checked.

1   What was the original purpose of publishing incoterms? (1.8)

2   List the 11 incoterms, and classify them into two categories. (2.6)

3   The EXW term is the one that imposes the greatest level of responsibility on the seller. True or false? (2.10)

4   Explain what is meant by FOB. (2.13ff)

5   Explain what is meant by CIF. (2.29ff)

6   Explain what is meant by DDP. (2.44ff)

11

CHAPTER 12

The Transport of Freight

Assessment criteria and indicative content

2.3 Describe the use of warehousing equipment
- Palletisation and unit loads
- Packing and packaging

3.4 Develop a plan for the transport of freight
- Arranging the purchase or export of cargo
- The role of freight forwarders and customs agents

Section headings

1 Unitisation and containerisation of loads
2 Intermodal transport
3 Freight forwarders and customs agents
4 Logistics and the environment

1 Unitisation and containerisation of loads

1.1 The unit load concept comes from the realisation that one of the areas of high cost in logistics comes from the inefficient handling of many small packages. The unit load enables goods and packages to be grouped together and further handled and moved effectively using mechanical equipment.

1.2 The two main unit loads are the wooden pallet and shipping containers. In essence these carry out the same functions through being of standard sizes although the pallet is designed to fit in the container. The challenge is to choose the most appropriate type and size of unit load in order to minimise the frequency of material movement and reduce costs by speeding up handling times.

1.3 There are many occasions where the container itself is the unit load. Containers are of standardised sizes and can carry equal weights. Shippers therefore know what they will carry and shipping lines, port authorities and logistics operators have the infrastructure in place to manage them.

Unitisation of loads

1.4 A unit load is an assembly of individual items or packages, usually similar in type, which enables convenient movement of goods. Pallets that enable movement by forklift are the most common and come in a wide variety of formats: wood, plastic, shrink-wrapped, strapped and roll-cage pallets are examples. ISO containers also represent unit loads. They may contain palletised or individual freight inside but they move as one integral unit.

1.5 Here are some of the benefits of effective unitisation of loads.

- Moving maximum quantities per journey
- Minimising individual movements
- Additional security
- Better use of space
- Ability to use standard handling and storage equipment
- Less handling
- Reduced pilferage
- Easier transfer from transport to warehouse.

1.6 Companies using ISO containers, as an example, will seek to maximise the numbers of goods they can physically place in a container. This can affect all sorts of decisions: are the benefits of washing powder in tablet form really the result of 'cutting-edge' marketing, or could the main benefit be that more actual product can be fitted into an individual container, thereby reducing the number of deliveries that need to be made?

1.7 The unit load concept is widely utilised in the physical movement of goods enabling the use of standard equipment irrespective of use. The benefits of standard equipment can be seen in warehouse design where racking is purpose designed to facilitate storage and easy movement of unitised cargo. Unit loads themselves vary considerably to suit individual requirement but meet industry standards.

Containerisation

1.8 International Standards Organisation (ISO) containers are designed for the movement of freight. They come in a range of types including:

- end-loading with a hard top
- end- and top-loading with a canvas top
- end-, side- and top-loading with half-height size walls
- insulated and refrigerated (reefers)
- liquid containers within a container frame.

1.9 There are many variations to suit individual movement requirements. Standard ISO sizes in common usage are 20-foot and 40-foot containers.

1.10 Road haulage has specialist vehicles designed to securely move standard 20 foot and 40 foot containers. Much of the movement involving containers is principally carried on 'swap bodies', a system that involves demountable load carrying units that are transported on flat or skeletal trailers by road and on specially designed flat platforms by rail.

1.11 The unit load concept is an integral part of the storage and distribution function. Containers can be easily delivered using a range of transport modes. Internally the use of unitised packing maximises efficiency in loading and/or unloading, vehicle turnaround times and product protection. Industry standards ensure consistency on an international scale.

2   Intermodal transport

2.1   Combinations of transport modes (also known as 'intermodal transport' or 'multimodal transport') are now an integral part of the movement of goods. As an example, a shipment by container from London to Nairobi might travel by road to an inland clearance depot (ICD), by rail to the port, by sea to Mombasa, by rail to Nairobi, and by road to the customer's premises. Specialist companies and shipping lines have taken the lead in developing these combined operations. The logistics manager needs to consider alternative routings, security implications and handling facilities.

2.2   The growth in intermodal transport has occurred alongside the acceptance of containers. The following definition of intermodal transport is from the European Council of Transport Ministers: 'The movement of goods in one and the same loading unit or vehicle, which uses successively several modes of transport without handling the goods themselves in changing modes'.

2.3   Intermodal transport involves the carrying and movement of freight using specially designed carrying and cargo protecting units that can be easily swapped between several transport modes such as sea, road, rail, inland waterway etc. This approach avoids unloading and reloading of individual items but results in a lower overall payload owing to the duplicated load-bearing elements of the rail vehicle and the load carrying units.

2.4   As a transport system, intermodal business tries to combine the benefits of various transport modes to achieve an overall gain. As an example, goods being delivered for seafreight will be delivered to an ICD in advance of the arrival of the vessel. In the majority of cases these containers will be moved by rail to the port where they may be moved by road alongside the vessel before being loaded on board.

2.5   Each transport mode has its own set of rules and regulations. These clarify the legal obligations of both shipper and carrier. Among other areas they state the amount a carrier is liable for in case of loss or damage. This differs with each transport mode.

2.6   When using intermodal transport the lead carrier, often the shipping line, acts as a **combined transport operator** who will usually offer remuneration to the higher level of the transport modes on offer. The shipper or consignee would be expected to insure the cargo according to the incoterm applicable and make any claim accordingly. The insurance company would meet a legitimate claim but, in turn, will claim against the combined transport operator.

2.7   Documentation has been revised to meet the requirements of combined transport. Traditionally, bills of lading (in essence the master transit document for sea-freight consignments) operated on a port-to-port basis. When containerised transport became increasingly important a document that allowed for transit from, for example, the exporter's premises to the destination country's ICD or through to the customer's premises was required. This place-to-place bill of lading is known as a **combined transport bill of lading**.

2.8   Development in intermodal transport has been rapid in recent years with a growth in specialised handling equipment to enable transfer between the different transport modes. Handling equipment must be able to raise and lower containers. Such equipment is large in size and requires considerable investment.

12

Intermodal transport and the supply chain

2.9 Intermodal transportation provides a flexible response to changing supply chain management requirements in global markets and logistics. The integrating of transport modes requires a process or systems approach and an in-depth knowledge of the supply chain and logistics process.

2.10 An integrated intermodal transport system is a significant and critical factor in the successful delivery of supply chains. Options in the intermodal link in supply chains are being heavily driven by information and communications systems.

2.11 Customers of global supply chains in the future will continue to demand faster supply chain delivery of their goods. Speed of total transit time through the supply chain will continue to be a necessary factor of intermodal transport. Customers will also have more access to information than in the past, and that information will drive higher expectations of performance as well as providing the foundation for alternatives, options and change.

2.12 Intermodal transport is seen as a significant and critical factor among supply chains in the future. Government support is driving the industry forward. Greater emphasis is being placed on training and awareness. Global companies who understand and integrate intermodal transport and systems into their supply chain process will be well set to look forward with confidence.

3   Freight forwarders and customs agents

Freight forwarders

3.1 A freight forwarder, as the name suggests, is an organisation assisting in the movement of freight across international boundaries. The freight forwarder is an intermediary between exporter and importer.

3.2 The freight forwarding industry can provide a range of key services to traders, taking over on your behalf many of the responsibilities involved in transporting your goods around the world as quickly, securely and affordably as possible.

3.3 As well as arranging the transport of your goods – whether by air, sea, rail or road – freight forwarders frequently provide other services in areas such as customs clearance, export documentation and insurance. They often offer distribution, warehousing, packaging and other supply chain services. Most forwarders will take over specific parts of the process for you, and can often offer control of the entire transport process. Many transport and logistics operators also offer freight-forwarding services.

3.4 Freight forwarding has developed into a highly professional and competitive business area that can provide cost savings, when using consolidation (air) or groupage (sea) services together with the specialised skills and knowledge of the forwarder in a range of ancillary areas.

Exporting

3.5 In the current trading environment many freight forwarders include value-added services such as data transfer, cargo tracking (track and trace), implants, project agency, global forwarding management etc. The integrated services offered and the increasing effectiveness of technology have led to considerable developments in this business area over recent years.

3.6   The forwarder is the link between the buyer and the seller and their ability to deliver services as promised is crucial to the perception of an exporter in the eyes of his customer.

3.7   Key areas that forwarders will offer include the following.

- Consolidation and/or groupage services. One of the main advantages of using a freight forwarder lies in the ability to group together consignments from several exporters and present them to a shipping company or airline as a single large consignment. The increased buying power of the forwarder is reflected in cost reduction to the shipper. The principle of consolidation enables the forwarder to offer added value to the shipper. A forwarder will consolidate in one country and despatch the consignment to an associate or subsidiary forwarder in the destination country. The destination agent will break down the consolidation, clear customs and deliver to the final customer as required by the exporter.
- Payment of freight and other charges. When a normal trading relationship has been developed the forwarder will accept charges on behalf of his clients. An exporter requiring the services of airlines, shipping companies etc together with transportation, packing, handling, insurance etc, can arrange to receive only one invoice from the forwarder.
- Ancillary services. The forwarder can offer a wide range of support (covering areas such as packing, warehousing, inventory control, documentation) that serve to provide an integrated logistics approach which can satisfy any requirements that a customer may have.

3.8   According to Alan Branch (*International Purchasing and Management*) the freight forwarder has four prime activities.

- He provides a range of services such as packing, warehousing, port agency and customs clearance.
- He provides advice on the transport of international consignments.
- He acts as an agent on behalf of either exporter or importer, organising transport or shipping space on their behalf.
- He acts as a multimodal transport operator in his own right, conveying from exporter to importer or for some part of that journey.

Importing

3.9   The main function for the forwarder or customs broker is to obtain clearance of goods through Customs authorities and deliver them to the customer. The main areas involved are as follows.

- Notification of arrival is given to the consignee by the carrier. If the consignee has appointed a forwarder to represent them that advice will be given to the named forwarder. The forwarder will then act on instructions from the consignee.
- Customs clearance. All goods entering the country are required to be declared in full detail, in the prescribed manner, to the Customs authorities. Customs have responsibility for collecting import duties and other charges due in accordance with law. Rates of duty are fixed according to the item involved, its origin and its intended use.
- Payment of taxes, duty and other charges. One of the major benefits for a trader is the ability to co-ordinate payment of the various elements involved in the importation. This may avoid the importer needing to arrange bank guarantees for payments or needing to establish separate accounts with carriers, ports and clearance depots. The freight forwarder can arrange for these charges to be presented as one account.
- Delivery, storage and distribution. As the import clearance agent collects from the shipping line or airline it is a logical development that they should offer a range of services for

12

the handling and delivery of the cargo. All aspects of delivery can be arranged to suit the importer's needs.

3.10 As far as importers are concerned a synopsis of the freight forwarder's role is as follows.

- He notifies the importer of the arrival of goods and advises on the necessary documentation for securing customs clearance.
- He organises customs clearance for the consignment.
- He organises payment of taxes and other charges on behalf of the importer.
- He organises onward transport of the consignment to the importer.
- He breaks bulk and distributes to his various principals.

Customs agents

3.11 Customs agents and customs brokers fulfil similar roles to each other and the terms are often used interchangeably.

3.12 While a freight forwarder will arrange for your goods to be transported from one country to another and typically provide other services as well (such as customs clearance), customs agents and brokers make sure that your goods can be cleared through customs *en route* to the final place of delivery.

3.13 Agents and brokers usually operate as direct representatives, but they can also act as indirect representatives. A direct representative acts in your name and can't be held liable for your customs debt. An indirect representative acts in their own name but on your behalf. They can be held liable for your customs debt.

4 Logistics and the environment

4.1 The area of 'green logistics' is one that is of growing importance and one about which both shippers and carriers are becoming more concerned.

- For shippers the concern is that goods should be carried in environmentally efficient transport modes that limit environmental damage as much as possible.
- The carriers look to minimise fuel usage by use of efficient vessels, aircraft or vehicles both to reduce cost and as a marketing tool to both shippers and the public.

4.2 Sea freight goes largely without notice unless a disaster at sea strikes. Vessels are designed to be fuel-efficient and operate to obtain the maximum fuel usage commensurate with a reasonable delivery time. Emphasis has been placed on increasing vessel size without increasing pollution levels. In reality this is partly an environmental consideration and partly an economic decision.

4.3 Air transport causes noise pollution and road bottlenecks at airports, and has high fuel-burn in comparison to other transport modes. Road and rail are more visible and come under closer scrutiny.

4.4 Logistics is a contributor to economic growth in two main areas.

- Efficient logistics extends market reach, by giving manufacturers access to a wider range of raw materials and supplies. Logistics in its widest sense also includes the distribution of information and related services, increasing the value even more.
- Efficient logistics reduces waste, both in production and in the use of capital.

4.5   Improvements in logistics have reduced physical waste, particularly where stocks are perishable. On a wider scale logistics has facilitated substantial reductions in working capital tied up in stocks in the economy, allowing the money to be diverted to more productive uses. During the past 10 years, the ratio of manufacturing stocks to output has fallen by over 20 per cent.

Road haulage

4.6   Alongside growth and increased professionalism the role of transport has undergone a quiet revolution. We have seen the development of regional, national and global 'hub and spoke' distribution networks that allow for smaller consignments to be consolidated into full loads. There are also considerable gains to be made by the application of technology that enhances the entire storage and distribution sphere of operations.

4.7   Vehicles have become more fuel-efficient as governments continue to raise duties but also because efficiency gains are at the heart of logistics thinking. Alternatives to the traditional diesel fuel – such as liquid petroleum gas or liquid natural gas – are being used where appropriate. Legal constraints on emissions drive higher environmental standards. ISO 14001 places environmental concerns on supplier and hauliers together, and as the haulage industry works more closely on environmental issues with suppliers the gains should be more than worthwhile.

Benefits of reducing vehicle emissions

4.8   Limiting vehicle emissions can reduce environmental impacts. Emissions from vehicle exhausts are a significant source of air pollutants including:

- CO_2
- carbon monoxide
- fine dust particles
- nitrogen oxides
- unburnt hydrocarbons.

4.9   Logistic operators will try to limit the amount of vehicle emissions that your business produces as they may lead to ill health, such as respiratory problems, among your staff and the public, cause a nuisance to your neighbours, contribute to roadside levels of pollution in urban centres and contribute to climate change

4.10   A logistics provider can project an improved business image by reducing its environmental impact. It can help to demonstrate corporate social responsibility as awareness of environmental issues is growing, and customers, investors and other stakeholders increasingly prefer to deal with businesses that have good environmental credentials. Having environmental policies and procedures and/or attaining an environmental accreditation such as ISO 14001 demonstrates an environmental commitment and is likely to be viewed positively and help win contracts when tendering for business.

4.11   Purchasers will usually include environmental issues as they carry out supplier appraisals and it is not only the supplier that may be appraised, it can also be their business partners who form an integral link in the supply chain.

12

Chapter summary

- A unit load is an assembly of individual items or packages which enables convenient movement of goods.
- Containerisation means the transport of goods in standardised containers.
- Intermodal transport describes the use of different transport modes to move goods from their origin to their destination.
- Freight forwarders provide a range of services to assist both exporters and importers in the transportation of goods across international boundaries.
- The role of a customs agent is to ensure that goods are cleared through customs.
- Environmental concerns are increasingly important in logistics and transportation, both as a means of saving costs, and to improve public image.

Self-test questions

Numbers in brackets refer to the paragraphs above where your answers can be checked.

1   Why do we practise unitisation of loads? (1.5)

2   List types of ISO containers. (1.8)

3   What is meant by a 'combined transport operator'? (2.6)

4   Describe the role of a freight forwarder in assisting (a) an exporter and (b) an importer. (3.7, 3.10)

5   Why are environmental concerns becoming more important for both shippers and carriers? (4.1)

6   Suggest benefits of reducing vehicle emissions. (4.8)

Subject Index